Alpine Level II Study Guide

Alpine Level II Study Guide

Professional Ski Instructors of America Education Foundation

CREDITS

Education Director
Linda J. Crockett

Technical Editor
Weems Westfeldt

Cover Illustration/Design Standards
Lee Reedy Creative

Graphic Design/Pre-press Production
Ken Grasman

Digital Photo Design
Boulder Media Group

Photography
Scott Markewitz

Still Images
Rodnunsky Arts, Ltd.

ISBN 1-882409-l0-8

Table of Contents

Acknowledg-ments

The PSIA Steering Committee developed the concept of presenting the American Teaching System alpine information as an assortment of materials. The pieces of the system manual, study guides, video, and handbook work synergistically to produce a complete picture of an effective alpine lesson.

- The *Alpine Manual* covers the American Teaching System, the role of PSIA in the ski industry, and a variety of subjects that contribute to the working knowledge of ski instruction.
- The study guides available for Level I, II, and III instructors contain the step-by-step procedures for conducting a ski lesson. They are written to be useful for the instructor who teaches, or is preparing for certification, at that level.
- The *Alpine References* video runs parallel to the content in the manual and study guides. It provides moving images of the skiing discussed in the ATS publications and was the source of most of the photos.
- The *Alpine Handbook*—a pocket-sized guide—contains exercises and drills that can be used with any level of class to develop improved learning and skills acquisition.

The study guides were co-authored by David Mannetter and Nancy Oakes of the PSIA Alpine Demonstration Team. These individuals drew upon insights, ideas, and their personal experiences to describe how to present an excellent ski lesson. Reading the study guides is like taking a private lesson with one of these accomplished skiers. David and Nancy set a fine example of teamwork in producing the study guides.

Pat Butowick, ski instructor at Heavenly Ski Resort and technical writer/editor, developed the study questions relating to each chapter of the study guides. She painstakingly distilled the key points to provide a valuable tool for study and discussion. In true PSIA spirit, Pat always provided what was required, plus a little extra.

Weems Westfeldt, a former member of the PSIA Alpine Demonstration Team, and currently a trainer with the ski schools of Aspen, served as technical editor for the study guides as well as the manual. Weems worked 25 hours a day to accomplish this task.

Bill Grout, senior executive editor for *SKIING* Magazine, read through the study guides and constantly challenged us to provide technical information in skier-friendly terms.

The PSIA Alpine Demonstration Team developed the core of ideas presented in this edition. The team is instrumental in PSIA's educational process and provides a constant source of creative energy.

The PSIA Board of Directors supported the project both in encouragement and funding.

The review panel for this publication consisted of the following individuals, who offered valuable advice:

Jack Copeland
Johanna Hall
Megan Harvey
Glen Peterson, Ph.D.
Sue Spencer
Calvin Yamamoto

PSIA instructors are also acknowledged, because it is you who can take the words on these pages and transform them into memorable experiences for your students.

Linda J. Crockett
PSIA Education Director

Study Guide Organization

This study guide contains suggested progressions for Levels 4-6, or intermediate phase skiers. It provides step–by–step suggestions for helping your students acquire the skills they need. Each level builds on the successes of the previous level—moving from simpler to more complex.

Sample progressions and progression options are provided for each level. These are followed by a technical summary of skill development appropriate to that level.

Following the concepts, you will find questions and answers for checking your understanding. Plus, notes pages are interspersed for listing your own progressions and other pertinent information from your ski school training.

Intermediate phase skiing covers a great deal of material. The information given for any level is not necessarily intended to be covered during one class. With help from the trainers at your resort, it is up to you to decide which lesson plans to use, based on the current skills, expectations, and goals of your students. Your decisions will also be influenced by weather and snow conditions.

The steps outlined in this study guide are only one set of teaching possibilities. Use your judgement, experience, and creativity to help you choose what, how, and when to use any of this material. Further, use this information as a foundation to develop your own progressions. Challenge yourself, when you read a progression involving one type of skill use or performance zone, to create your own teaching patterns involving alternative skills or performance zones.

The *Alpine Level II Study Guide* corresponds with the *Alpine Manual*. You can refer to the manual whenever you need background information about the Skiing Model, which is the basis for the concepts and progressions in this book. The following list describes where you should look in the manual to find specific information that supports this study guide.

Level 4 Skier: see Chapter 4, The Skiing Model, Level 4, (Wedge Christie; Balancing, Rotary, Edge-control, and Pressure–control Movements)
Level 5 Skier: see Chapter 4, The Skiing Model, Level 5, (Wedge Christie; Parallel; Balancing, Rotary, Edge-control, and Pressure-control Movements)
Level 6 Skier: see Chapter 4, The Skiing Model, Level 6, (Parallel; Balancing, Rotary, Edge-control, and Pressure-control Movements)

Note: As you work with any of the materials in the American Teaching System, you may come across unfamiliar ski terminology. Please refer to the glossary and/or text of the *Alpine Skiing* manual for explanation of these concepts. Ski instructors use terms in a variety of ways, so in any technical discussion, always state what you mean and ask others to do the same.

While the use of ski terminology is an effective way to communicate with other instructors, you will want to develop non–technical translations of these terms for students.

Skier Level 4

Exploring Natural Snow Conditions and Matching the Skis Earlier in the Turn

Lesson Outcome

Students learn to apply their skills to a wider variety of snow conditions and terrain. Through a slightly earlier weight transfer, they learn to ski wedge christie turns with less effort.

In Level 3, students learned to vary the size and shape of their wedge turns. Turn shape variety is a hallmark of increasing proficiency. They also learned the fundamentals of matching and skidding and began to explore very basic sideslipping and shaping the bottom of the turn with a blend of skills using an uphill christie. These students are now ready to apply their skills to new terrain and different snow conditions (photo 1). During this phase, concentrate on applying and anchoring what your students have already learned rather than on trying to rush them on to more advanced movements or mechanics.

Refresher Run

1. Begin by reviewing your students' ability to link wedge turns. Many of these students may not have skied for some time. Ski at least one warm–up run on groomed green terrain. For the first few turns, it is probably best to have them follow you in a line. Lead them

Photo 1. Apply Skills to New Terrain and Snow Conditions

first through a series of medium turns, with consistent turn shape and rhythm as goals.

2. As they show competence and confidence with these turns, gradually begin to vary the turn shape by changing the timing. You can lead them into shorter turns without saying anything at first. By steering more actively for a shorter period, your wedge turns will become a little smaller. Your students may not notice at first, but they will be able to follow you into these shorter wedge turns.

3. When you stop after a series of turns, point out to your students the way they were able to change the shape of their turns as they skied behind you.

4. Ask the group if anyone would like to verbalize what he or she did differently to make the turn quicker. Be careful, though, not to put any one person on the spot. If no one is able to describe the differences, you can quickly tell them about

guiding their skis more actively from one turn to the next.

5. Next, ski a few turns that are less finished and stay more in the fall line.

6. Without stopping, ski some very round turns that go more across the hill.

7. Again, during a short rest period, discuss the differences in execution and sensations of these two different turn shapes. All of this can easily be done on the first run.

8. During the first run, you should also review inside leg steering and the sensation of allowing the skis to skid as you steer them through the bottom part of the turn. Emphasize pressure on the outside ski during the last third of the turn in both demonstrations and in your descriptions and instructions. As you move the group down this first run, continue to reorganize them so every student has a chance to ski behind you and get the best view of what you are doing.

New Snow or Powder

Introducing your students to natural snow conditions gives them the opportunity to apply their present skills to new situations and to gain sensations that may be different from those they have experienced so far. Skiing in new snow provides new sensations, and through this process your students begin to expand their skill base (the available combinations of movements).

If possible, take your students to a green run somewhere on your mountain that has some powder or ungroomed snow on it. Remember that this will be a completely new and perhaps frightening experience for them, so ski on terrain with a pitch that will not intimidate them.

1. Explain that matching the skis in this snow condition is less important than just linking wedge turns.
2. Emphasize strong, continuous steering to keep the skis turning through the greater resistance offered by the fresh snow.
3. Explain that their speed won't increase because of the resistance of the deeper snow, and that skiing a slightly straighter turn shape enables them to move more easily from turn to turn.
4. Without presenting any more information, lead them through a series of turns. By leading, you will be able to demonstrate the turn shape and degree of finish. Six or eight turns should be enough to provide an opportunity for your students to try this without becoming overwhelmed.

Photo 2. Extension and Flexion in a Wedge-christie Turn

5. Once everyone has successfully skied a few turns, select a stopping point that is a few turns further down the trail and give these students a chance to ski on their own (because if you continue to lead them in a line, they won't be skiing fresh snow). By keeping the skiing segments short enough, you assure that all students will feel they can successfully reach the stopping point.

Keep close track of each individual. Don't merely watch their turns, but also try to "read" their body language. Stiff or rigid legs and arms may be a result of fear. Acknowledge their fear, but do not dwell on it. Instead, give them a mechanical focus to occupy their attention. Stay close to those members of your group who seem apprehensive and assure them that you are there to help them.

If some of your students are still afraid, try asking them to squeeze the grips of their ski poles as they ski through the last half of a turn. This will help shift the focus of their tension to another part of their body.

Since you want them to be as relaxed as possible, ask them to relax their hands a little bit as they begin the next turn. This will help to relax their entire body. If necessary, allow them to squeeze their pole grips tightly once again during the bottom of the new turn. Soon, they will begin to relax and enjoy the new sensations of skiing fresh snow.

6. Once your students have skied a few turns, have them focus on a

more deliberate weighting or pressuring of the outside ski. Ask them to start the turn by "rising" (extending) and relaxing a bit as they steer both skis down the hill.

About the time they reach the fall line, show them how to press a little more on the outside ski as they continue to guide both skis through the bottom of the turn. The increased pressure will help engage the outside ski, and the interaction of the ski with the snow will combine with steering to bring both skis through the rest of the turn. Photo 2 shows extension and flexion in a wedge-christie turn.

As they increase pressure on the outside ski, most people also tip that foot, leg, and ski more. This movement engages the edge a little more, and the sidecut of the ski will also aid in the turn.

Relaxing the inside leg while pressuring the outside ski also contributes to an easy matching of the inside ski. Matching the skis in a turn can be seen in Photo 3. After more practice, the inside leg should not only be relaxed, but should also be tipped toward the center of the turn. At first, this occurs after crossing the fall line. As students gain experience, this matching occurs earlier in the turn. This tipping movement eventually becomes an active steering movement.

Spread the presentation of this information throughout the lesson, because mileage and practice are

Photo 3. Matching the Skis in a Turn

essential elements at this stage. Share your joy and enthusiasm for skiing in new snow as you provide guidance and coaching. As the lesson progresses, you may want to venture onto terrain that is slightly steeper. If you do, teach your students to apply a rounder, more finished turn shape to control speed.

Emphasize patience during turn initiation and strong, continuous activity throughout the turn. Table 1 discusses difficulties your students may experience in new snow or powder and how you can help.

Garlands

To help build confidence in your students, you can teach garlands as an exercise. As you know, garlands allow you to work on the top and bottom of a turn without actually having to cross the fall line.

1. On an easy–to–moderate slope, extend while steering both feet toward the new turn. The extension should be gradual and should last almost to the fall line.
2. Press on the downhill ski while flexing and steering the skis back across the hill.
3. Repeat two or three times across the hill, and in both directions.
4. Gradually steer the top of the turn further into the fall line before steering back across the hill.
5. Finally, make a full turn. Extend and steer into the fall line. Flex, press on the outside ski and continue to steer through the bottom of the turn.

Small Bumps or Rolls in the Terrain

Skiing over small bumps and/or rolls in the terrain will enhance your students' balancing skills and help them learn about changing their blend and application of skills. Like skiing in new snow (which is not always available), skiing over terrain variations at this level provides new sensations in skiing.

After an appropriate warm–up and review (as presented earlier in this section), take the group to a run that has not been groomed for a couple of days. The pitch of the terrain should be well within their capabilities. A green or very easy blue trail is just right.

Turning Around the Bumps

The objective for this learning segment is to develop your students' ability to feel an increase of pressure under the ball of the foot as the ski starts up the bump, and an awareness of the pressure moving throughout the foot from front to back as the ski travels over the bump.

1. Move your students to a low traffic area on the hill.
2. Ask them to focus on the sensations of pressure that they feel on the bottoms of their feet while skiing up one side of a mogul and down the other side.

   Make them aware that pressure on both the heel of the foot and the back of the boot cuff leads to being caught off–balance, with their weight on the backs of their skis.

   Encourage them to bend their ankles into the front of the boot cuff as the tips of the skis start up the side of the bump. Then, as their skis travel over the top and down the other side of the mogul, have them maintain

light pressure against the front of the boot. Gentle pressure on the front of the ski boot helps them maintain a centered stance over their skis. Keeping their hands loosely in front of their bodies will also help them remain centered.

3. Lead the group in a line for at least half a run while turning around the bumps. Ski over the bumps between turns and around the bumps while turning. Select a turn shape that is open enough so that students are not forced to turn more quickly than is comfortable. This practice time will give the students time to anchor the sensations and mechanics of remaining centered as the skis encounter variations in the terrain. By not actually having to turn on a bump while focusing on balance, students quickly learn to adapt their stance to the bumps and rolls.

Turning over the Bumps

When the students seem fairly comfortable skiing across bumps and turning between them, they are ready to start turning over the bumps.

Remember, these terrain variations should not actually be moguls—simply very small variations in the snow surface.

1. Lead the group (in follow–me formation) in a short series of six or eight turns, initiating the turns on bumps or rolls. Try to time it so that the point of matching corresponds to the

Table 1

New Snow or Powder		
Problem	Possible Cause	Solution
Student cannot initiate a turn in the deeper snow.	1. Leaning in the direction of the next turn, which takes too much pressure off the outside ski, making it very difficult to start the turn. 2. Student may be trying to pivot or twist the skis too quickly at the start of the turn. 3. Student may be frightened of the snow condition and/or terrain.	1. Make sure that the student is balanced on both feet at the top of the turn. 2. Emphasize patience when initiating the turn and gradual, continued steering throughout the turn. 3. Take the group to flatter terrain to rebuild confidence, then gradually increase the level of challenge again.
Student has difficulty finishing the turn.	1. Not enough pressure on the outside ski. 2. Student may be skiing stiffly.	1. Increase pressure on the outside ski starting in the fall line. This increased pressure will help to build better ski-snow interaction so the student's efforts to steer the ski are transmitted correctly. Make sure the student is not leaning toward the center of the turn. 2. Emphasize flexion during the second half of the turn. Flexion and extension movements will aid in adding rhythm to the students' skiing. Progressive flexion will provide more steering power because more leverage is applied as the leg is bent.
Student crosses ski tips while turning.	Often caused by steering only the outside ski, leaving the inside ski literally in the way of the outside ski.	Emphasize inside leg steering throughout the turn.

crest of the bump.

As they come over the top of the bump they will already have a little pressure on the front of the ski boot from flexing while matching the skis. As they encounter the crest of the bump, they should also actively be guiding their inside ski, foot, and leg. They will soon realize that the terrain makes matching easier, and should feel fairly comfortable turning over the bumps because of the practice they got skiing across bumps (between turns).

Matching Skis in Bumps

To reinforce the ability to match the skis in this terrain, or if some students are having difficulty dealing with the rolls and matching at the same time, spend a little time with a static exercise to review the movements of matching.

1. Stand on top of a roll with your ski poles anchored for balance.
2. Demonstrate how easy it is to steer your inside foot and ski by twisting and slightly tipping your leg.
3. Give each student the chance to try the same movement.
4. Make a turn over one bump, demonstrating the same inside leg activity to match the skis while coming over the top of a bump. Let each student try this activity in one turn.
5. Link turns together over a series of rolls to reinforce the timing and movements of matching in this terrain situation.

Uphill Christies with Appropriate Edge Engagement

Students at this level are ready (and need) to learn to edge their skis more actively after matching. This will require them to deliberately tip their feet and legs inward. If they make this movement in conjunction with their flexion, a smooth, progressive edge engagement will result. Teach or review uphill christies to provide appropriate edge engagement.

1. Start at the side of the trail. While standing in place, demonstrate progressive flexion while tipping the ankles and knees into the hill. Explain that this movement will cause the skis to come up onto their edges and that the design of the skis will help create the bottom part of the turn.

   Demonstrate this movement as you ski from a shallow traverse while skiing toward your group. Draw attention to the way your skis tend to pull through the bottom part of the turn.
2. Let your students try this movement one at a time, in each direction.
3. Gradually work the starting point a little closer to the fall line.
4. When everyone in the group can successfully execute uphill christies in both directions, incorporate uphill christies into a turn by using that movement to make the very last part of the turn.

Uphill christies will help students at this level understand how they can effectively use more active edging to help shape the bottom part of the turn. This movement will be especially useful in turning over and around rolls in the terrain and in very small bumps. As they continue to develop as skiers, students learn that this fundamental exercise is effective in a wide variety of situations!

Developing an Earlier Match

You will find that most students learn to match earlier with little guidance from an instructor simply through mileage and practice time. This natural development can be facilitated by focusing on and practicing the movements and timing of matching.

Matching the skis higher in the turn will require an earlier commitment to the new outside ski and a more actively steered inside ski. Developing these two elements will result in a more efficient and less fatiguing turn for your students. In the process, balance and ability to move from ski to ski will develop. Active movement from one ski to the other is an important point in the student's development because it represents one of the fundamentals of advanced skiing.

Thumper Turns

To help students develop better pressure control over the outside ski during their turns, teach them to make thumper turns. (Children, or the young at heart, can relate this exercise to the Disney character "Thumper the Rabbit").

1. Describe thumper turns for the group. The idea is to tap or thump the inside ski on the snow during the last part of the turn. This will guarantee proper weight distribution because you will not be able to lift the inside ski unless you are balanced on the outside ski.
2. On gentle, smooth terrain, demonstrate a thumper turn coming toward your group to provide the best view. As you ski through the last third of the turn, actively flex over the outside ski as you tap or thump the inside ski on the snow two or three times (see photo 4, thumper turn).
3. If there are no questions about the exercise, demonstrate a thumper turn again, this time skiing away from the group.
4. Have each student practice this exercise one at a time.

    They may have difficulty performing the exercise the first time through. Provide encouragement and comment on the positive elements of your students' performance while offering corrections, if necessary.
5. When every member of the group has tried the exercise, have them incorporate it into a series of turns where each turn is finished with a few thumps during the last third (or so) of the turn.

    You can have students practice the exercise as a group, or provide some open practice time. Open practice would consist of allowing each person to ski his or her own pace while practicing instead of leading them in a line. This type of class handling can be an effective means of helping students become more self-sufficient on the mountain.
6. As the group becomes more comfortable with the exercise, you can encourage an earlier commitment to the outside ski by asking them to start thumping the ski a little earlier.

    Instead of waiting to exit the fall line, ask them to try to start thumping the ski as they enter the fall line. Emphasize progressive flexion on the outside ski and leg as they thump the inside ski. This will aid both balance and the ability to continue steering the inside ski as they increase pressure over the outside ski.

    Explain to the group how thumping the inside ski should allow them to feel more pressure over the outside ski during the turn. Point out how the thumping action also makes the inside ski easier to steer because there is so little resistance to guiding it.
7. When your students can comfortably execute thumpers, take them back into a skiing segment where they no longer lift the inside ski off the snow. Instead, tell them to make the inside ski light as though they were going to thump it. The ski will remain on the snow, but will still be easy to steer because it is so light. Spend at least one entire run focusing on this before moving on or ending the lesson. The longer the practice session, the sooner a new movement can become an integral part of an individual's skiing.

Photo 4. Thumper Turn

Skating

If the terrain is very flat, or if your group seems to be quite athletic, try teaching skating in addition to thumpers. Skating is an excellent way to develop active movement from one ski to the other. It also helps develop edging skills and the ability to generate forward glide on very flat slopes.

Demonstrate skating and then have your students practice it.

1. On very gentle terrain, glide on one ski for two or three ski lengths; then glide on the other ski.
2. Next, while sliding forward, push off of one foot onto the other. Slide for a few feet as you flex.
3. Push off of that foot and ski and onto the other while extending. Glide on the new ski while flexing again.
4. If your students find that their outside ski tends to slip sideways and away, remind them to tip the foot, ankle, and knee toward the other foot to engage the edge before pushing off of the old ski.

Specific Skills for Negotiating the Mountain

Students at this level are becoming mountain skiers. They need specific tactics and skills to help them move efficiently, comfortably, and safely from one place on the mountain to another—on both flatter and steeper terrain.

Sideslipping, traversing, and hockey stops can help them negotiate steeper sections and stop quickly.

Sideslipping

Students can use sideslipping to effectively lose elevation on hills they find a little too steep. They can also use the skidding that they learn from sideslipping to control their speed during the finish of their turns. Their skis will slow down due to the increased friction with the snow.

Take your group to the side of the trail or somewhere else out of the flow of traffic.

1. From a static position, describe, and demonstrate how to extend in the ankles, knees, and hips to flatten the skis.
2. Then have the group try the movement along with you.
3. Next your students can point their skis downhill just enough to begin moving. Be sure they are in a flexed position as they begin to slide. Have them extend while continuing to slide forward on the snow. The tips of the skis will begin to point slightly farther down the hill. Then have them simply turn back into the hill to stop.
4. They should try this in both directions across the hill.
5. Show your group how to roll or point the ankles and knees slightly more down the hill while extending. This will flatten the skis even more, and allows the skis to drift both forward and laterally.

6. The students can then repeat this in the other direction.
7. Allow them to practice this forward sideslipping enough to become at least somewhat comfortable with it. If possible, have them try it on a small roll or other variation in the terrain that is steeper than the surrounding terrain. Explain the situations in which sideslipping is useful.

Traversing

Similar to the movements required for uphill christies, traversing requires the student to engage the edges by tipping the feet, ankles, and knees into the hill. This fundamental edging movement makes the skis bite into the snow so that the skis track instead of slipping or drifting sideways. Skiing in a traverse is shown in photo 5. The basic difference between uphill christies and the edging movements required for traversing is simply the degree to which the legs and skis are tipped. To traverse, the feet and legs need to be tipped only enough to get the edges to engage and hold, but not so much that edge angle continues to increase during flexion.

1. At the side of the run, demonstrate how to tip the feet and ankles into the hill while maintaining a fairly tall stance. You can visually highlight this point by asking the students to first watch your ankles and then your skis. They will be able to see the ski tip onto its edge.
2. Give everyone a chance to try the movement while standing in place. Be sure to have them

practice in both directions.

The goal is to make the skis grip so that there is no loss of elevation while skiing across the trail. Make a game of the traverse by challenging the group to see who can leave the clearest set of railroad tracks in the snow as they ski across the hill.

3. Ask the group to try to ski to a specific spot on the other side of the run (such as a tree or sign) by engaging their edges and traversing.

Explain that traversing will give them a means of getting around on the mountain more easily and without having to climb or hike as often. Both traversing and sideslipping are also an excellent means of adjusting their position in moguls. In order to establish or change where students are traveling, the skis can be engaged (to go above a mogul or other obstacle), or released to slip below or around a mogul.

Hockey Stops

While controlling speed with turn shape is (or should be) the goal of most good skiers, the ability to stop quickly is also a necessary skill. A quick stop makes skiing into lift lines or merging trails easier and more comfortable. Hockey stops enable students to stop quickly.

1. From a shallow traverse, demonstrate rapid flexion while twisting your feet and skis into the hill.
2. Have your students try the same movement. Emphasize the need

Photo 5. Traversing

to maintain pressure on the front of the boot during flexion to stay centered over the skis.
3. Have your students practice in both directions.
4. Gradually move the starting point deeper into the fall line, but avoid having your students go straight down the hill as this may intimidate some members of the group.
5. When the students are reasonably comfortable with the flexion and twisting movements, add a little more inward tip of the feet and legs to the twisting (steering) movement. This engages the edges more positively, and will result in a very quick stop.
6. Lead your group through a series of three turns.
7. After the third turn, finish with a hockey stop. It may be helpful to count backward on each turn, "Three, two, one, stop!"

8. As you continue to ski with your group, occasionally execute a hockey stop to reinforce the "on demand" nature of the movement.

Teaching specific tactics will give your students tools that will help them move around the mountain more easily and effectively. It is especially important to explain why you are teaching these movements, and to help students learn where and how to apply them! In this way, we can teach students to achieve tangible, useful results for a lifetime of skiing.

Note: Provide warning that you are about to execute a hockey stop to prevent your students from running into each other. Saying something like, "After the next turn we'll use a hockey stop," should provide adequate warning.

Technical Aspects of Skill Development

Balancing Movements

Reinforcing flexion and extension movements promotes balance by lowering the center of mass during the turn. The flexion and slight pressure on the front of the ski boot while skiing small bumps and rolls also promotes a centered stance. As these students gain experience in varied snow conditions, they learn more effective balancing movements.

Rotary Movements

At this level, steering is developed during flexion. As the leg is bent (during flexion), more rotary power can be delivered through the femur. This is important because as the ski is tipped onto its edge, there is more resistance to guiding it. Flexing the leg provides the necessary power to keep the ski turning as the edge begins to interact with the snow. Inside leg steering is enhanced with repetition and terrain utilization (such as skiing over bumps and rolls) as well as when students learn to ski with more weight over the outside ski earlier in the turn.

Edge–control Movements

In natural conditions, such as powder and small bumps, relatively flat skis are desirable because they are easier to guide. As students steer their skis back across the hill during the second half of a turn, edge angle naturally develops. If the legs and feet are tipped inward, this further enhances edging activity. Uphill christies require active edging movements, while traversing teaches students how to regulate the amount of edging.

Pressure–control Movements

Pressure to the front of the boot and flexion in soft snow and during thumper turns are forms of pressure control relative to fore/aft balance over the skis. Thumping, or making the inside ski light during the turn, adds pressure to the outside ski—a form of lateral pressure control. Skating develops pressure from foot to foot and is an important fundamental of upper-level skiing. The sooner weight is transferred completely to the outside ski during the turn, the earlier the skis can be matched. Pressure control is further developed as students learn to ski in small bumps because they become more sensitive to the sensations in their feet.

Level 4 Questions: Exploring Natural Snow Conditions; Matching the Skis Earlier in the Turn

1. Circle the best choice:
    If you steer wedge turns more actively for a slightly shorter period of time, they will become (smaller) / (larger) in size.

2. Circle the best choice:
    Fresh snow offers (less) / (more) resistance than hardpack.

3. Choose the best answer:
    In fresh snow or powder, you should have your students:
    A. Complete their turns more than on hardpack
    B. Keep their skis in the fall line more than on hardpack
    C. Make exactly the same shape of turn as you would on hardpack

4. Circle the best choice:
    In new snow or powder, emphasize (a more gentle steering action) / (strong, continuous steering).

5. One disadvantage of leading your group in a line through the powder is mentioned in the study guide text. What is it?

    The students do not get fresh snow, you make a path for them.

6. Why does the study guide suggest having your students try to squeeze the grips of their ski poles through the bottom of a turn, and then relax their hands somewhat as they begin a new turn?

    It helps release tension in the rest of the body, if the student is nervous.

7. Choose one or more of the following:
    During a lesson in new snow or powder, when you have your students slightly increase the pressure on the outside ski during the bottom of the turn, some will also slightly increase the amount they tip that foot, leg, and ski inward. This movement will cause:
    A. The edges to engage more
    B. The skis to slip more
    C. The skis to turn too far back up the hill

8. True or false:
    Relaxing the outside leg while pressuring the inside ski during a turn will contribute to matching.

9. Circle the best choice:
    In new snow or powder, leaning in the direction of the next turn will (increase) / (reduce) the pressure on the outside ski. This change in pressure will (make it easier) / (make it more difficult) to initiate the new turn.

10. Choose one or more of the following:

When teaching your Level 4 students to initiate turns in powder, encourage them to:

A. Pivot or twist their skis

B. Use patience

C. Sit slightly back

D. None of the above

11. What effect, if any, does progressively flexing during the second half of a turn have upon steering?

_____ Gives the student more steering power. _____

_____

12. Circle the best choice:

If your students are having difficulty making the second half of a turn in powder, have them (decrease) / (increase) the pressure on the outside ski starting in the fall line.

13. (True) or false:

Steering only the outside ski when turning in powder can be lead to crossed ski tips.

14. Choose the best answer:

A garland is:

A. A series of direction changes that eventually cross the fall line

B. A series of direction changes that do not cross the fall line

C. A series of slides directly down the fall line

15. Choose one or more of the following:

In the exercise where you have students ski up one side of a bump and down the other side, try to have them:

A. Feel gentle pressure under the ball of the foot as the ski starts up the bump

B. Feel gentle pressure under the heel of the foot as the ski starts up the bump

C. Maintain light pressure against the front of the boot as they travel over the top and down the bump

D. Maintain light pressure against the back of the boot as they travel over the top and down the bump

16. (True) or false:

As your Level 4 students encounter the crest of a bump, they should actively be guiding their inside ski, foot, and leg.

17. Choose the best answer:

You should exercise the most patience during turn initiation:

A. In the bumps

B. In powder

C. On steeper terrain

18. True or false:
    At this level of skiing, you want to encourage a passive movement from ski to ski.

19. Choose one or more of the following:
    Thumper turns:
    A.   Require your students to be balanced over their inside skis while tapping their outside skis
    B.   Require your students to be balanced over their outside skis while tapping their inside skis
    C.   Help develop better pressure control
    D.   Promote earlier matching

20. Choose the best answer:
    Open practice is:
    A.   A practice period of indeterminate length
    B.   A practice session where each person practices on his or her own
    C.   Practice time on an open hill

21. Choose one or more of the following:
    Skating helps develop
    A.   Matching
    B.   Edging
    C.   Gliding

22. Give a step–by–step description of skating at Level 4:

    _____

    _____

    _____

    _____

23. Choose the best answer:
    Your beginning skating student tries to push off of a ski but finds it slipping sideways and away.
    Prior to trying to push off of that ski, the study guide suggests that you tell your student:
    A.   To tip that foot, ankle, and knee more to the outside
    B.   To tip that foot, ankle, and knee toward the other foot
    C.   To move the center of mass over the other foot

24. Choose one or more of the following:
    Which of the following skills can help your students negotiate steeper sections of the mountain?
    A.   Diverging parallel turns
    B.   Sideslipping
    C.   Skating
    D.   Traversing

25. What effect does skidding the skis through the finish of the turn have upon the student's speed?

It helps bleed off speed, slows them down in a gradual, controlled manner.

26. In sideslipping, what happens to the skis when you extend in the ankles, knees, and hips?

they release the edges and start slipping down the hill. They flatten and slide.

27. What will happen to your skis if, instead of simply extending your ankles, knees, and hips to sideslip, you also roll or point your ankles and knees slightly more down the hill?

The skis will go slightly forward and laterally

28. The following statements describe either 1) traversing, 2) sideslipping, or 3) both. Write one of those three words next to each statement to identify it:
   A. An option (options) for students at this level who want to adjust their position in the moguls.

   both

   B. The feet and legs need to be tipped only enough to get the edges to engage and hold.

   traversing

   C. Learning this/these will enhance the skidding of the skis through the finish of the turn.

   sideslipping

   D. Teach(es) students about releasing the edges to allow the skis to drift.

   sideslipping

29. Choose the best answer:
   Which of the following results in the quickest stop:
   (A.) Hockey stops
   B. Sideslipping
   C. Sneak turns

30. Read the following excerpt from the Level 4 hockey stop progression described in the study guide and then answer the question which follows:
   1) From a shallow traverse, demonstrate rapid flexion while twisting your feet and skis into the hill
   2) Next teach your students how to increase the amount they tip their feet and legs into the hill
   In # 2, above, what should happen to their skis' edges when students increase the amount they tip their feet and legs into the hill?

   The edge should engage more fully.

31. Read the following descriptions of movements and skills that were introduced or refined during the Level 4 lesson and then write the name of the fundamental skill primarily involved. (Fundamental skills: Balance, Rotary, Edge Control, Pressure Control)

Note: If part of the description has been bolded, write the name of the fundamental skill which primarily applies to that portion of the description.

A. The flexion and slight pressure on the front of the ski boot while skiing small bumps and rolls also promotes **a centered stance**.

_____ Balance _____

B. At this level, **steering** is developed during flexion.

_____ Rotary _____

C. Tipping the legs and feet inward during the second half of the turn.

_____ Edging _____

D. Relatively flat skis are desirable in natural snow conditions such as powder and small bumps.

_____ Edging _____

E. **Inside leg steering** is enhanced with repetition and terrain utilization (skiing over bumps and rolls).

_____ Rotary _____

F. What skill besides balance is primarily involved in **maintaining pressure on the front of the boot in small bumps and rolls?**

_____ Pressure _____

Level 4 Answers: Exploring Natural Snow Conditions; Matching the Skis Earlier in the Turn

1. *Smaller.* If you steer your wedge turns more actively for a slightly shorter period of time, they will become somewhat smaller in size.

2. *More.* There is a little *more resistance* from fresh snow than hardpack.

3. B. In fresh snow or powder, you should have your students keep their skis more in the fall line.

4. *Strong, continuous steering.* In new snow or powder, emphasize *strong, continuous steering* to keep the skis turning because there is a little more resistance from the snow.

5. They won't be skiing fresh unpacked snow. If you continue to lead your students in a line during a powder lesson, they won't be skiing fresh snow.

6. Relaxes them as they begin their new turn—takes their minds off of fear throughout the turn. Having your students squeeze the grips of their ski poles through the bottom of a turn and then relax their hands somewhat as they begin a new turn gives fearful students a mechanical focus to occupy their attention, thus taking their minds off of their fear. When they relax the grip somewhat, they relax the whole body.

7. A. Tipping the outside foot, leg, and ski back up the hill at turn completion will engage the edges a little more. The sidecut of the ski will also aid in the turn.

8. *False.* Relaxing the *inside* leg while pressuring the *outside* ski will contribute to an easy matching of the inside ski. After more practice, the inside leg should not only be relaxed, but should also be tipped toward the center of the turn.

9. Reduce, make it more difficult. Leaning in the direction of the next turn in new snow or powder can take too much pressure off the outside ski, making it very difficult to start the turn. Make sure students who are having this problem are balanced on both feet at the top of the turn.

10. B. To teach your students to turn in powder, emphasize patience when initiating the turn and gradual continued guidance throughout the turn. Pivoting or twisting the skis too quickly at the start of the turn can lead to difficulties initiating the turn.

11. *Provides more steering power.* Progressive flexion provides *more* steering power because more leverage is applied as the leg is bent.

12. *Increase.* Have students who are having difficulty making the second half of a turn in powder increase the pressure on the outside ski starting in the fall line. This increased pressure will help to build better ski-snow interaction so the student's efforts to steer the ski are transmitted correctly. Make sure the student is not leaning toward the center of the turn.

13. *True.* Often, steering only the outside ski leaves the inside ski literally in the way of the outside ski, leading to crossed ski tips. Try emphasizing inside leg steering throughout the turn.

14. B. A garland involves a series of direction changes which do not cross the fall line. Garlands allow your students to work on the top and bottom of their turns.

15. A & C. In the exercise where you have students ski up one side of a bump and down the other side, they should feel gentle pressure under the ball of the foot as the ski starts up the bump and they should try to maintain light pressure against the front of the boot as they travel over the top and down the other side of the bump. This stance (aided by hands that are held loose and in front of the body) will help them to remain centered.

16. *True*. As your Level 4 students encounter the crest of a bump, they should actively be guiding their inside ski, foot, and leg.

17. B. You should exercise more patience during turn initiation in powder or deeper snow.

18. *False*. At this level of skiing, an *active* movement from one ski to the other is an important point in the student's development because it represents one of the fundamentals of advanced skiing.

    Matching the skis higher in the turn requires an earlier commitment to the new outside (turning) ski and steering the inside ski more actively. Learning this develops balance and the ability to move from ski to ski.

19. B, C, & D. The idea of a thumper turn is to tap or thump the *inside* ski on the snow. (For children, this exercise can be related to the Disney character, "Thumper the Rabbit"). This exercise will guarantee that the students have their weight properly distributed because they will be unable to lift or tap the inside ski unless their balance is focused on the outside ski (thus developing better pressure control over the outside. This exercise also promotes earlier matching and helps develop better pressure control over the outside ski during the turn.

20. B. Open practice consists of allowing each person to practice a specific exercise on their own. This type of class handling can be an effective means of helping students become more self-sufficient on the mountain.

21. B & C. Skating develops active movement from one ski to the other, *not* matching skills. It also helps develop edging skills and develops the ability to generate forward glide on very flat slopes.

22. The following is a step–by–step description of skating at the Level 4 level:
    1. On very gentle terrain, practice gliding on one ski at a time. Sliding for two or three ski lengths will be sufficient. Practice this on each foot.
    2. While sliding forward, push off of one foot and onto the other. Slide for a few feet as you flex.
    3. Push off of that foot and ski and onto the other while extending. Glide on the new ski while flexing again.

23. B. Remind beginning skating students who find that their ski slips sideways and away when they try to push off of it to first tip that foot, ankle, and knee toward the other foot to engage the edge.

24. B & D. Sideslipping and traversing will help Level 4 students negotiate steeper sections.

25. Slows the skier down. The skidding which Level 4 students learn from a sideslip increases the friction between the skis and the snow, slowing the skier down. This helps Level 4 students *control their speed* better.

26. *Flatten—and slide.* In sideslipping, extending in the ankles, knees, and hips flattens the skis, which then slide down the hill.

27. Will flatten the skis even more and will allow them to drift forward and laterally. Rolling or pointing the ankles and knees slightly more down the hill while extending in a sideslip will flatten the skis even more than extending alone would, and allow the skis to drift both forward and laterally.

28. A: both, B: traversing, C: sideslipping, D: sideslipping

    Your students will find that both traversing and sideslipping are an excellent means of adjusting their position in moguls.

    To traverse, the feet and legs need to be tipped only enough to get the edges to engage and hold, but not so much that the edge angle continues to increase during the flexion.

    Learning to sideslip will enhance the skidding of the skis through the finish of the turn.

    Sideslipping teaches students about releasing the edges and allowing the skis to drift both forward and laterally.

29. A. Hockey stops give students the ability to stop quickly. This is especially helpful when coming into lift lines and when merging with another trail.

30. They should engage more positively. Having your students tip their feet and legs inward more while twisting the feet and skis into the hill will engage the edges more positively, and will result in a very quick stop.

31. The primary fundamental skill for each selection (paying particular attention to the italicized portion) is:
    A. Balance: the flexion and slight pressure on the front of the ski boot while skiing small bumps and rolls also promotes a *centered stance*.
    B. Rotary: at this level, *steering* is developed during flexion. Flexing the leg provides the necessary power to keep the ski turning as the edge begins to interact with the snow.
    C. Edging: tipping the legs and feet inward during the second half of the turn.
    D. Edging: in natural snow conditions such as powder and small bumps, *relatively flat skis* are desirable because they are easier to guide.
    E. Rotary: *inside leg steering* is enhanced with repetition and terrain utilization (skiing over bumps and rolls).
    F. Pressure Control: *maintaining pressure on the front of the boot* in small bumps and rolls.

Notes:

Skier Level 5

From Wedge Christie to Beginning Parallel: Exploring Blue Runs and Varied Snow Conditions

The information and progressions contained here cannot necessarily be taught in one lesson. This covers a considerable amount of information—with help from the trainers at your resort, it is up to you to decide which lesson plans to use, based on the current skills, expectations, and goals of any given group. Your decisions will also be influenced by snow conditions and weather considerations.

Lesson Outcome

Students learn to ski most blue runs and use appropriate tactics for different snow conditions. Students gain balance, rhythm, and timing of movements by learning to plant their poles and match their skis in a parallel relationship early in the turn (advanced wedge christie and beginning parallel).

Compared with Level 4 students, Level 5 skiers are ready to ski more of the mountain, including steeper slopes and easy moguls as well as more difficult snow conditions (such as powder, crud, and ice). To match the skis in the first half of the turn, students need to become comfortable skiing at slightly higher speeds than they are used to and to transfer their weight to the outside ski earlier in the turn.

Terrain

Choose a low intermediate (easy blue) run for your warm–up run.

Class Arrangement and Handling

Before you start down a run, consider your options of either leading the group through the first few turns, or of selecting and identifying a place to regroup. If your first run is in a high traffic area, it may be safer to lead the group. If you lead, you need to watch the individuals in your class over your shoulder to make sure that they are in the right class, and to assess their current skill levels. Be careful not to allow the movement of your head to affect your body position as you demonstrate—a challenge for every demonstrator!

Allowing your students to ski on their own at this point makes it much easier to watch them during their first few turns. Consult your ski school trainer to determine which method is preferred in your ski school.

Reviewing Wedge–christie Turns

During the warm–up run, assess the current skills of your group and review their ability to comfortably start to match and skid somewhere around the middle of the turn (at or just past the fall line). During the first stop, quickly review
- the centered stance.
- steering with the feet and legs.
- inside leg steering to match the skis.

It's very possible that some members of your group will not have made a warm–up run on their own, or may not have skied at all since their last ski trip. This makes the initial run quite important, so do not rush your group through this stage.

While reviewing the basic mechanics, provide individual feedback to the students: let them know individually what they have done well, and where they should focus their attention and efforts during the next skiing segment. Now you are ready to continue with the warm–up run. In most cases, plan to devote an entire run to warming up.

Different Turn Shapes and Sizes

For these students become more well–rounded skiers, and to ski comfortably on more of the mountain than they can currently handle, they need to be able to vary the sizes and shapes of their turns. They also need to be able to make both shallow turns (i.e., less-finished, linked turns that keep the skier moving across the fall line), and complete turns that cross the fall line. To help them develop versatility and an understanding of what shape of turn works best in a given situation, explore a range of turn shapes and sizes— from shorter to longer and from fall line to across the fall line finish. At this level, most students use steering to change the size and shape of their turns.

Shorter, Crescent–shaped Wedge-christie Turns

Steering more actively with both feet and legs during the initiation of a turn creates a shorter turn shape. Lead your group through this progression on moderate (easy blue) terrain:

1. Demonstrate a series of turns where the main focus is on actively twisting both feet as you ski in a wedge. Using a taller stance will help keep your skis flatter in the snow and will make them easier to steer.

2. As the turn develops, continue to guide both skis in the intended direction while flexing your knees and ankles. For now, you should flex more over the outside ski to keep from over–edging on somewhat flatter terrain. Over–edging will hamper your ability to complete the turn. As you begin to flex (roughly when your skis are in the fall line), you should have completed transferring your weight to the new outside ski. You will probably match the inside ski to the outside ski at about the same time.

As speed control is not an issue (because the terrain you selected is gentle), extend and steer quickly. This initiates the turn just as soon as your skis have turned away from the fall line. The goal is to work toward a shorter, crescent–shaped turn without sacrificing the ability to match the skis. Allow students enough practice time to become comfortable with the idea of staying in the fall line while guiding

Photo 6. Creating a Rounder Turn Shape

their skis from one turn to the next. Point out how the short, round, but unfinished shape of this turn results in speed maintainance, while still providing control. The fact that this turn allows the skis to continue gliding well on the snow makes it appropriate for flatter sections of any mountain.

Gliding Medium–radius Turns

To create a gliding medium-radius turn, apply the same idea of actively steering with the feet and legs. The medium-sized turn will require students to be a bit more patient as they steer into the turn. The goal here is simply to change the timing of movements the students already know how to do.

1. Demonstrate a longer turn by steering slowly and patiently through the entire turn. Actively flex and extend in these turns, but execute the turns from a somewhat tall stance (just as in

the shorter turns) to help keep the skis fairly flat. The shape of this turn should still be kept close to the fall line, without traversing, to maximize gliding of the skis.

2. When you have shown a few of these turns, invite the group to practice some as well. They will learn that the steering activity of the turns is not changed, and that only the amount of effort required and the timing are different (i.e., less effort is required because there is more time to turn the skis). Explain that these gliding turns are a good choice on terrain that is fairly flat because they keep the student from losing too much speed.

3. On steeper terrain, without changing the focus, demonstrate a few turns where you start to round out the shape of the turn by continuing to steer the skis back across the fall line (See Photo 6).

Runs that are steeper demand

a more finished turn shape to keep your students from going too fast. Here again, the timing of the flexion and extension movements is a little different. Demonstrate that, by continuing to flex and steer, you turn further back across the hill.

4. Ask your students to ski a series of turns in which they steer back across the hill, just as you did in your demonstration. All they need to do is continue to guide their feet and legs in the intended direction.

During this process, ask them to be aware of the sensation of slowing down as they come back across the fall line. Be sure that all members of your group understand that this continued steering is what controls their speed. As the skis come across the hill, more edge angle and pressure naturally develop on the outside/downhill ski, which combines with steering to help round out the bottom of the turn.

As edging and pressure increase, extension becomes more important. This is because extension helps release the edges and allows your students to steer their skis more easily. For this reason, be sure to encourage the members of your group to make a good extension movement as skis open into a wedge.

Varying Turn Shapes and Tempo

A playful session in which you have students vary the shape of the turn helps develop the ability to change the size and shape of the

turn on demand. The terrain should still be somewhat moderate, alleviating fear. This is another situation where you will most likely want to lead so you can dictate the transitions from one turn shape and size to the next. If you have a student who is having difficulty, put that person in line behind you to provide a clear view of what you are doing.

1. Lead the group through a fairly long series of turns, beginning with a round, speed–controlling, medium duration turn. After a few of these, when everyone is comfortable with the rhythm, try the following: quicken the turns by steering more actively. If this causes too much slowing, encourage students to stay closer to the fall line.
2. Slow down the pace of steering to make more of a medium–paced turn.
3. Gradually add more guidance through the bottom of the turn to create a more finished turn shape, which slows the group down. Were they aware of the increase of speed with shorter turns? Did they find that the next set of turns (medium, but close to the fall line) were also fast? What changed to slow them down again before they stopped? Guide a discussion with the students to help them understand what happened.

Building an awareness for the students helps them understand how to make appropriate choices for themselves later on. Explain again that the roundest, most finished turn shape is most appro-

priate for steeper terrain, and that the more open, gliding turns work well on flatter terrain.

Improving Flexion and Extension Movements

Flexion and extension movements are essential to good pressure control and effective skill blending, plan to spend time developing an appropriate range of motion. More dynamic flexion and extension movements promote earlier matching, as well as weight transfer, and pressure control over the outside ski. Demonstrate two to four turns where you exaggerate the flexion and extension movements, and ask your students to exaggerate the range of motion, also. Most people feel that they are moving up and down (flexing and extending) more than they really are. If necessary, demonstrate what you see them doing, then ask them to try again.

To help your students get a feeling for the timing of these gradual (and continuous) rising and sinking movements, try this exercise.

1. Demonstrate a round, finished medium turn while counting out loud to a three–count while extending, and then once again while flexing, as follows:
- On 1, start to extend.
- On 2, after having initiated the turn, continue to extend.
- On 3, when you are almost in the fall line, come to the peak of your extension.
- Repeat the three–count while flexing and finishing the turn. Your flexion should be at the

same rate as your extension.

2. Ask your students to count to themselves as they attempt to match what you have just shown them. (They will feel much less self–conscious if they count to themselves than if they count out loud.) It may be unrealistic to expect your students to perfectly match their movements to the count, but it helps them understand that the extension should last almost to the fall line, and that flexion lasts throughout the second half of the turn. As with any exercise that you introduce, provide practice time.

Developing Active Skill Blends: Sideslipping Progression

So far, students have improved flexion and extension movements and active steering skills. As the students become more competent with these movements, you should begin work toward developing an active blend of skills during the turn. Try teaching sideslipping to review edge-control skills. This exercise develops simultaneous (same time and same direction) use of both feet, ankles, and legs. These simultaneous movements are an important building block as students move toward parallel turns.

1. From a static position with your skis across the hill, demonstrate how to release the skis' edges by relaxing your legs and rolling the ankles and knees slightly down the hill. The action of rolling the ankles and

knees during a turn was evident in photos 2 and 3.
Hold your hands quietly in front of your body to promote good balance and body position. As your edges release their grip in the snow, your skis begin to slip laterally. After you have slipped a few feet, gradually tip your feet, ankles, and knees back into the hill to engage the edges again and come to a stop.

2. Have your students practice this a few times on each side. Have them strive for a balanced stance so that their skis slip sideways down the hill, as directly as possible. They should focus on feeling the whole bottom of the foot inside the ski boot to keep centered while slipping. If their skis move diagonally forward while slipping, they are probably leaning a little too far forward. If the tips of the skis start down the hill while the tails remain more engaged, there is a little too much weight on the heels. Students at this level may not yet have the sensitivity to stay perfectly centered, but they will gain much in the process of trying!

3. Link flexion and extension movements to sideslipping by having them extend as they roll their knees and ankles down the hill, and flex as they re–engage their edges.

4. If combining all of these movements immediately seems like asking too much, have the students make a few turns focusing on rolling their legs down the hill while rising; then have them

make a few more turns focusing only on rolling the legs back into the hill while flexing and steering. After that, the whole package can be reassembled!

Relate this exercise to the big picture by asking your students to apply what they have just practiced to their skiing. Be sure to provide plenty of clear demonstrations to reinforce what you are saying.

Skating

Skating is an excellent exercise for improving flexion and extension. As students begin to explore a broader spectrum of runs on the mountain, skating also makes them more mobile, and can be used to develop active weight transfer and independent leg movement.

Skating is worthy of being repeated in many levels of student development. It is introduced at an elementary level in Level 4, again here in Level 5, and will be used again in Level 6. Students stand to gain much experience and understanding about edging and pressure control from skating.

If the terrain is flat, you may want to teach the following progression close to the fall line. If the terrain has a bit more pitch, teach this progression more across the hill. Start in a position facing your group.

1. From a flexed position over one ski, describe and demonstrate how to push off from that ski forward and toward the other ski. This movement propels you forward. To push off from a ski,

it must be edged. Be sure to actively extend while pushing off from the ski.

2. As weight settles on the new ski, allow that ski to glide a few feet as flexion begins. Roll the ski onto its edge during flexion by using the ankle and knee. Emphasize light pressure on the tongue of the boot to stay centered.

3. Repeat these movements as you push back to the original ski.

4. Repeat the demonstration, this time going away from the group. Try to skate from foot to foot at least two or three times without stopping.

5. Give your students the opportunity to try skating on their own and then together with you as a group. The most common problem or difficulty for students results from a lack of edge engagement, or from standing too tall and without sufficient flex in the ankle. Emphasize tipping the leg inward to edge the ski during ankle flexion.

Matching Earlier in the Turn

Now that you have built the fundamentals, your group can continue working toward parallel turns. One of the main factors that helps students match their skis higher in the turn is earlier weight transfer, and the first steps toward that objective are to narrow the wedge and increase speed. Narrowing the wedge and increasing speed coaxes students to commit themselves to the outside ski higher in the turn to maintain balance and control. It is

effective because your students will experience an earlier weight transfer, although they may not yet know how or why!

Approaching the lesson in this way is a form of the guided discovery teaching style. This style is characterized by leading your students through a series of steps or exercises so that they discover an outcome on their own—even though you knew all along what they would find.

Continue skiing on easy blue terrain, but, if possible, ski a different trail. This adds variety to your lesson and acquaints students with more of the mountain. In many cases, students find it very easy to successfully narrow the wedge if you simply ask them to do so. If the terrain is too steep, though, the chances for success are reduced.

1. Describe and demonstrate a smaller wedge.

2. Demonstrate the relative size of the wedge openings your students currently use.

Seeing the difference between what they are doing and what you want them to do will help them to progress more rapidly. Again, narrowing the wedge is the first step, even if they continue to maintain the wedge until after the fall line at first.

3. Ski a segment to allow students to practice these smaller wedge openings.

Many students will continue to use the wedge even though they don't need to. This may simply be a habit, or it may be that they are intimidated by in-

creased speed.

4. If they are achieving a smaller wedge, but not matching earlier, start to focus on inside leg activity.

Explain that by making a smaller wedge, the inside leg is in a better position to be steered to parallel. Point out how, as they extend and steer into a wedge, both knees tip toward the turn's interior. By rotating the inside foot and knee further toward the center of the turn, that inside ski will pivot easily on the snow. This is especially true if the inside ski is fairly light (due to a shift of most of the weight to the outside ski).

5. To emphasize this point visually, ski a couple of turns toward the group and at a somewhat slow speed. Ask them to watch your feet and knees during this demonstration. Ski the demonstration all the way to the group. They should have noticed the movements and the narrower relationship of your feet and legs. Check for understanding by asking someone to describe what they saw.

6. Have the group try three or four turns executing this combination of movements. Rather than calling the students down one at a time, ask each person to start after the person in front of them has made two turns. This puts you in a position to watch the first person, then provide feedback while watching the second person, and so forth.

7. Once everyone is successful, a practice session is in order. Choose a point somewhere

down the trail to regroup, and space the group on the hill by having the second person start skiing after the first has made two or three turns. This form of class handling allows you to roam through the group, watching and providing encouragement and feedback while they are skiing. Allow the group plenty of time to make a number of turns and get a feeling for the combination of movements. Gauge the fitness levels of the students to prevent them from becoming tired too quickly. This portion of the lesson will take at least a whole run, perhaps more.

Note: If the entire class is successful, you can move on to the next progression. If not, provide feedback and corrections, and try again. It is more important to continue to practicing the correct movements than to move on quickly.

8. At the next stop, ask if anyone was aware of increasing weight on the outside ski earlier than they did when the matching occurred after the fall line. Most likely, someone will have noticed that to steer the inside ski sooner, their weight had to be committed to the outside ski higher in the turn. If no one noticed, take the opportunity to explain it to them.

9. To drive the point home, have the group make a few turns, lifting the inside foot slightly as they steer it to a matching relationship.

Using Garlands to Enhance Inside Leg Steering and Edging Movements

You can focus on inside leg steering using a more step-by-step approach if the group needs it. This garland exercise enhances the activity of inside leg steering and helps anchor the earlier weight transfer and commitment to the outside ski at the same time.

1. Start in a shallow traverse across the hill, with skis in a slight wedge.

2. Demonstrate (toward the group) how to actively roll the inside knee and ankle into the hill while maintaining pressure and balance on the outside/downhill ski. Explain how this movement corresponds to matching and to sideslipping (the action of tipping the leg is similar to what happens when the inside leg is steered to match the skis during a wedge–christie turn, and is the same as engaging the edge of the inside ski in sideslipping). Your students will not be able to tip the inside leg unless they are balanced over the outside/downhill leg and ski.

3. Flex and extend several times.
   - Each time you extend, your ski tips will start down the hill.
   - Each time you flex and tip your inside leg toward the hill, your tips stop drifting down the hill and begin turning back uphill.
   - This produces the garland shape.

4. Demonstrate while going away from the group: flexing and tipping the inside leg into the hill, then extending again. Repeat this movement two or three times as you ski across the hill.

5. Ask your students to execute the movement that you just demonstrated. This may be awkward for them during the first few tries. Be patient and provide plenty of encouragement and feedback.

6. Repeat the exercise in the opposite direction.

7. Lead the group through a series of wedge–christie turns using this very active inside leg movement to match the skis.

Once students are comfortable matching their skis higher in the turn, they can begin to explore how edging skills fit into more advanced wedge–christie turns.

1. Have your students ski another series of turns which you initiate with a narrow wedge opening and during which inside leg steering occurs above the fall line.

2. After matching the skis, demonstrate an inward movement of the knees and hips during flexion. Demonstrate this first moving toward the group, and again moving away.

3. Have the students use this movement as they ski through a series of turns. It creates a blend of edging and pressure control that influences the second half of the turn. As the edges are engaged more actively, the shape of the turn becomes more sharp and clean. Rather than skidding

and drifting during the second half of the turn, the skis begin to slice through the snow with more grip. The turn is still round, but the bottom is sharper than it was without active edging.

Uphill Christies

After using garlands to further develop inside leg steering, you can once again use uphill christies to help students develop more active edging skills. Start on an easy blue run and at the side of the trail. Ski down and across the hill at approximately a 45° angle. Demonstrate and then have your students practice the following:

1. From a tall stance, flex your ankles and knees slightly forward and inward to tip the skis up onto their edges. This should be a progressive movement that engages the edges gradually. The hips should remain over the feet, with the hands comfortably up and in front of the body.

    As the skis begin to bite into the snow, the design of the ski causes them to climb back up the hill in a shallow turn.

2. Execute this maneuver two or three times in each direction, each time skiing farther down the hill and closer to the fall line before flexing back into the hill.

3. Incorporate the uphill christie movements into turns. After you have matched your skis, flex slightly forward and maintain pressure against the front of the boots. The skis slice through the bottom part of the turn with very little effort from the student.

Next, have your students try these activities.

1. Have them practice tipping the skis onto their edges after the match.

2. When they can competently perform this movement, have them begin to explore ranges of edging. In some turns, have them tip their ankles and knees very slightly into the turn. Point out how the shape of the turn becomes somewhat elongated.

3. In other turns, have them tip their knees and ankles more aggressively toward the inside of the turn. Point out how the finish of these turns becomes significantly shorter and tighter.

4. Next, take the group to a blue run that is slightly steeper than the one on which you have been practicing, or to a run that has some slightly steeper sections so that they can apply their edging skills to steeper terrain.

5. Lead the students in a line to set the appropriate turn shape. By following you at first, students are able to focus on executing the movements. Remember to take it easy on the first few turns because the situation may be intimidating for some members of the group.

    Your students already know (from turn shape work) that steeper terrain requires them to ski their turns back across the hill (finish turns) enough to control speed. Edging throughout the second half of the turn helps accomplish this by reducing the amount of skidding during the turn. By combining active edging with continued steering of the feet and skis, the design of the skis helps to finish the turn back across the fall line and control speed.

6. Have them practice on their own for a while. This type of practice is very valuable because it helps them to become more self–sufficient as skiers.

7. Have your students begin to increase the inward movement of the outside leg during flexion to increase the edge angle and bite of the skis. By increasing the edging activity in the second half of the turn and actively steering at turn initiation (and throughout the turn), your students achieve a fairly short turn with good skill blending.

Note: Terrain selection is important. If the terrain is too steep, fear may become a disruptive factor. When students become fearful of the terrain, or of falling, ability to concentrate on the task is greatly diminished.

Introducing the Pole Plant

An effective pole plant is an important aid to timing and balance, and makes skiing in ungroomed snow (powder and moguls) easier and more comfortable. For most students, learning to plant their ski poles can be a challenge. Be prepared to spend at least a couple of hours on teaching pole action. Try not to get frustrated if other aspects of performance decline in the process: focus on one thing at a time (teaching an effective pole plant) and address other problems later.

Hand Position

The first step in introducing a solid pole plant is to make sure students have good hand position. If they do not, spend some time with the following progression to develop it.

1. Describe the desired hand and arm position. The hands should be comfortably up and in front of the body. As a rule of thumb, the elbows should at least as far forward as the sternum, and the hands should be just above the waist.
2. Statically, have your students place their hands and arms in the position you've just described while holding onto their poles.
3. Ask them to engage the pole tips in the snow by pressing the heels of their hands forward.
4. To anchor an awareness of this hand position, ask the group to traverse across the hill while continuously pressing with the heels of the hands to get the pole tips in the snow. Have them try to leave two distinct lines in the snow (from the pole tips).
5. It may be helpful to ask your students to imagine that they are carrying a tray with cups of water on it. Tipping the tray to either side or downward will spill the water.
6. Have them ski a series of turns while dragging the pole tips, trying to leave lines in the snow.

Photo 7. Pole Plant

Pole Swing and Touch

Hand position is an important factor in learning to plant one's poles, but the act of swinging the ski pole tip and touching it in the snow usually requires very specific practice. Explain that the tip of the pole should be planted in front and somewhat to the side of the student's boots. As a visual reference, the pole should enter the snow somewhere downhill of the front third of the ski. If the pole is planted too close to the skis, the student will be forced to ski past the pole tip before starting to turn. Therefore, there should be at least a couple of feet between the pole tip and the skis. The use of a pole plant to initiate a turn is shown in photo 7.

You are ready now to start teaching your students how to swing their ski poles.

1. Standing in place, ask your students to again hold their hands and arms in the position they have just learned. Ask them to hold their hands high enough so that the tips of the poles are free of the snow.
2. Show them how to use their wrists to swing the tip of one pole forward without changing the relationship of the hand, arm, and torso. Have them move their wrist so that their thumb moves toward them and the heel of the hand moves away from them. They will readily see how this movement

makes the tip of the ski pole swing forward.

3. Ask them to reverse the movement to swing the pole tip back again.

4. Have them repeat this movement several times with the same hand, then practice it with the other hand several times.

5. Now have your students try swinging the tip of one pole forward and, as it swings back, swing the other pole forward. They should continue to work both wrists so that both poles are moving constantly in opposite directions. The purpose of this is to help your students get the feeling of swinging both poles at the same time.

6. When they can consistently alternate pole swings, show the group how to plant the tip of the pole each time they swing it forward. The timing should be such that by the time one tip is being planted in the snow, the other pole is beginning to swing forward.

More Dynamic Pole Action

At this stage, your students are ready to start practicing a more dynamic pole plant. Use the following progression to provide the repetition that is so important in teaching and learning.

1. Have each person swing and plant the downhill pole three times (from the wrist only).

2. The third time they swing the pole, ask them to initiate a new turn. They should plant the

poles just before they match their skis so that the plant becomes a cue to match. The pole plant occurs in conjunction with the edge change because it is the least stable part of the turn. In this case, matching the skis constitutes the edge change.

3. While traveling in the opposite direction, ask them to repeat the three pole swings and plant. Again, on the third swing, have them start the turn.

4. If more practice is needed or desired, have your group reduce the number of practice swings before the turn to two. Otherwise, ask them to turn each time they swing the pole forward.

Try to establish a consistent rhythm so that the timing of each pole swing is the same as the last. A medium-radius turn is probably best, because it allows time for them to concentrate on their poles without having to rush into the next turn. Remember, this process will probably require quite a bit of guided practice time!

Students often become confused as they work on swinging and planting their poles. One common error at this stage is planting the wrong pole. The goal is to swing the right pole as a right turn is initiated, and the left pole for the left turn. If they begin to plant the wrong pole for a turn, stop them at that point to make the necessary corrections. It may be helpful to describe the pole as a turn signal. The right pole signals a right turn; the left, a left turn. Patience and understanding on your part will help your stu-

dents learn the correct movements. Keep close track of each individual's performance during this part of the lesson.

Another error that students commonly make when first learning a pole plant is to drop the inside hand after the pole is planted. This can be a problem because a low inside hand can lead to over-rotation of the body during the turn. Even if over-rotation is not a result, dropping the hand after the pole plant requires an extra, less efficient movement to prepare the pole for the next turn. Emphasize the idea of using only the wrist to swing the pole, and remind them of the tray with water glasses on it: they should try to hold their hands quiet to avoid spilling the water.

The Frog Hunting Progression

Learning pole action can be challenging, as previously stated. The more creative you can be in your teaching, the more likely it will be that your students will succeed. If you have an imaginative group of people, you may want to try the frog hunting progression.

1. Ask the students to imagine they are going frog hunting. Since frogs are only out at night, they will also need to imagine that they have a flashlight in their uphill hand. They will use the ski pole in their downhill hand to catch the frog.

2. While skiing across the hill, have them swing the pole forward so that they are ready to touch the frog with it when they

Photo 8. Timing the Pole Plant

A

B

C

shine the light on it.

3. With the uphill hand held forward (so that they can shine the light), ask them to touch the downhill pole and turn.

4. Now they must imagine that the light has switched hands. As they approach the next turn ("frog"), they should touch the new downhill pole and turn again.

Note: Regardless of the progression you choose to teach, be sure to allow plenty of practice time. Again, watch them closely; provide plenty of feedback, corrections, and encouragement!

Developing the Timing of the Pole Swing

Once the students are using correct pole action, explore how the timing of the pole swing changes relative to different sizes and shapes of turns. This is probably best done by simply describing what you want them to do in a specific turn, demonstrating, then practicing while skiing together. Photo 8 shows pole plant timing in a turn.

Pole Swing in Short Turns

1. Describe pole swings in short turns. The student should begin to swing the pole as soon as the turn starts. Waiting to swing the pole will result in a late pole plant and is ineffective as an aid to timing the turn entry. The edge change is usually the least stable part of the turn, so a late pole plant is of little use for balance during the turn.

2. Demonstrate the timing of the pole action in a short turn while skiing toward the group. The students are able to see pole actions best when you ski toward them.

3. Provide your students with free practice time (using task style teaching). Task style teaching is when you assign a task or activity to students—who are then given performance boundaries and are free to practice on their own. This makes it easy for you to watch each individual as they practice.

Pole Swing in Medium Turns

The timing of the pole swing for a medium turn is somewhat different than for a short turn. Because the turn itself is longer and takes more time, it is not necessary to swing the pole as soon or as quickly.

1. Ski toward your group to demonstrate the appropriate timing. While maintaining a good hand position, start to swing the pole for the next turn as you enter the fall line. Swing it slowly enough so that the movement lasts to the end of the ongoing turn, and so the pole plant corresponds with the initiation of the next turn. It is unrealistic to expect your students to perfect the timing for a medium turn, but an accurate demonstration will convey the idea that they should swing the pole a bit more patiently in a medium turn.

2. Spread your group out to practice so you can keep an eye on everyone.

3. After some practice time with

this slower pole swing in a medium turn, start to mix the radii of the turns between shorter and medium–radius turns. Not only will this reinforce the difference in timing of the pole swing, it will also serve as additional practice for the movements of the feet and legs.

Following Pole Swing to Develop Movement Toward the New Turn

A good pole plant enhances rhythm from turn to turn. The pole swing can also be an effective cue for directing extension movements down the hill and toward the center of the next turn. If the previous lesson plans have been covered, your students will be ready to start moving down the hill as they initiate a turn. This requires a change in the direction of extension movements and may be challenging for them.

Directing extension movements toward the downhill side (as opposed to only extending vertically) enables lateral movement that makes your students' skiing more efficient and contributes to more consistent motion from one turn to the next. This concept is commonly referred to as the "flow of the center of mass," (i.e., movement of the path of the body's center of mass), and becomes increasingly important as students develop and begin to ski more challenging terrain and snow conditions.

Teaching this more lateral pattern of movement requires creativity on your part and imagination on the part of your students. The basic idea is simple: as students swing their poles, they should try to move their hips in the direction they want their skis to go during the next few seconds. (Since the goal is get the ski tips going down the hill, this is also the direction they move their hips.) As they extend, ask them to try to push their hips slightly toward the next turn. Your students can imagine that there is a small rope between the tip of each pole and the adjacent hip. The rope is long enough for them to swing the pole without interference, but short enough that as they swing the pole, the rope pulls their hip in the same direction.

If you like, you can demonstrate and have your students practice this movement statically.

1. Start in flexed position, as though you have just finished a turn.
2. As you swing the pole, extend up, forward, and across the skis. Your hip should move enough for your skis to flatten and begin to slip downhill. Because you have moved forward as well, your ski tips should start down the hill and toward the top of a new turn.
3. Demonstrate this movement a couple of times statically, then show the same movement as you start a turn.
4. Call your students down one at a time to make sure they are executing the movement correctly (this is a visual check for understanding).
5. When they can execute the movement in each direction, have them put it into action while skiing through a practice segment.

Static Progression for Extension

A static exercise focusing on the direction of the extension and the resulting release of the edges is sometimes very helpful at this stage. For the moment, it may be best to focus on the extension movements and not worry about the pole swing because the pole swing can be added again at the end of this progression.

1. From a standstill at the side of the trail, place your skis into a small wedge, flexing your knees and ankles.
2. Demonstrate how to extend slowly and deliberately so that your hips gradually move up, forward, and slightly across the skis all at once. This slow extension releases the edges and allows the ski tips to begin drifting toward the fall line.

   Note that moving slowly is important because you want the skis to begin moving due to the edge release, rather than because of momentum generated by a quick extension, followed by a sudden halting of that movement.
3. Now ask your students to try the same movement. From a static position, they should start out flexed, and extend slowly forward, up, and across the skis. Provide plenty of encouragement, feedback and corrections. Above all, try to be patient because learning to move more

across the skis may take time!

4. When the students can get their edges to release from the static position, have them add the pole swing and plant again.

5. Have your students apply the same movements while skiing, starting first with just a few turns so that you can keep an eye on each student.

Applying Turn Shapes to Different Terrain and Snow Conditions

By now, your students have learned the skills necessary for skiing all blue runs. Guide them through an exploration of the mountain to anchor the use of different turn shapes relative to the terrain and snow conditions. Students at this level find that the pole plant is an aid to balance in all situations—particularly on steeper terrain, bumps, and powder.

Steeper Terrain

Your students have already learned how to control speed through the shape of their turns. Rather than leading them, allow them freedom to choose the shape and size of their turns. Emphasize pole use in this situation. Later, set a task for the group: ask them to ski a long series of turns where they vary the turn shape to go faster and slower during the run.

Take the class to trails that have terrain ranging from flatter to steeper. Challenge them to ski the runs at a constant pace. To achieve this goal, they have to change the shape of their turns as they make

the transitions between flatter and steeper terrain.

Small Moguls

Practice turns on runs that have small moguls or ski on the edge of a trail with bigger moguls. A blue run that was groomed the previous day will often provide this condition. Encourage your students to use a pole plant to help stabilize their bodies as they begin a turn on the top of a mogul.

Describe what to look for when selecting places to turn in the bumps: the top of each bump has a small flat spot. If they begin to turn on the flat spot, it is easier to steer into the new turn. Planting the pole on the flat spot helps them identify the correct place to initiate the turn and provides an aid to balance.

Point out how easy it is to steer the skis from the top of the bump. Flexion and extension movements help smooth out the terrain. The legs should be kept somewhat relaxed so that skiing over a bump does not push the students out of balance. The extension should be fairly slow to reduce the chance of losing ski–snow contact while skiing over the top of the bump. The flexion should also be gradual and progressive. This promotes good balance for the turn's finish. The movements of skiing through small moguls are depicted in Photo 9.

Powder

Deeper snow or powder will likely be more of a mental than physical challenge for your students. When introducing them to this snow con-

Photo 9. Skiing Through Small Moguls

dition, avoid taking them to a run with deep powder. Three to six inches of new snow would be ideal, but you may not be able to choose how deep the snow is. Often, during storms, new snow will accumulate during the course of your lesson. If you encounter this, make the most of it by teaching students to apply their current skills.

As with steeper and flatter terrain, success in skiing powder requires changing the shape of the turn. While on groomed terrain, a straighter turn shape (one that is closer to the fall line) is an accelerating turn; in powder, it is the turn shape that provides enough glide to make turn initiation easier. Deeper snow creates more resistance than packed snow, which means you will go more slowly in powder than on groomed snow. A round, finished turn will cause you to slow down too much and make it difficult to start the new turn.

Also, because of increased resistance, steering the skis in powder is more difficult than on groomed snow. Your students need to put more effort into their steering movements. Explain that the steering movements require more power, but should still be patiently executed.

Good flexion and extension movements help reduce the resistance between the skis and snow, and help provide the necessary increase in muscular power.

Note: Take the opportunity to discuss ski design as it relates to powder skiing. Encourage your students to try out skis designed especially for powder. This can add immensely to their enjoyment of powder skiing!

Hockey Stop Progression for Powder

1. Have your students start in a shallow traverse with skis parallel.
2. Once they are sliding, ask them to flex quickly and twist both feet and legs across the hill. Tipping the knees slightly inward helps both steering and edging. Tipping the legs also engages the edges and cause the students to stop quickly. Pressure and balance should be focused primarily over the outside/downhill ski.
3. Have them practice in both directions, progressively starting closer to the fall line. From the fall line, have them repeat the hockey stops, this time slowing the rate of both flexion and steering. The steering movement should last throughout the maneuver. As long as flexion is continuous, the students will be able to continue steering. Again, have them practice in both directions.
4. Once your students develop accurate timing of flexion and steering, demonstrate a progressive but deliberate extension which starts well before you have come to a stop. During the extension, open into a small wedge while steering both feet and legs into the new turn.
5. Work this exercise into a garland. Demonstrate how to extend and steer into the fall line, followed by flexion and steering back across the hill.

   Note that students often mistake quick steering for powerful steering. Steering quickly causes the skis to get caught in the powder, interrupting balance. Emphasize progressive flexion and extension movements, and steering during the range of motion (the flexion and extension movements).
6. Give students a chance to practice these movements.
7. Have your students ski a complete turn using the movements they just practiced in garlands.
8. Have them add an active pole plant to facilitate balance and to help stabilize themselves. Emphasize the idea of following the pole swing to move more toward the new turn. Getting the students to extend so that they move more across the skis than up will make it easier for them to maintain momentum between turns.
9. Practice, practice, practice!

Pedaling Progression for Powder

Focusing on the weight transfer will make it easier for your students to get to the fall line in deeper snow. To help your students develop an active, yet controlled weight transfer, use the analogy of pedaling a bicycle to get from one ski to the other.

1. Describe the action of pedaling a bicycle—you move pressure smoothly and gradually from one foot to the other. As the pedals turn, you apply weight to the new pedal at or near the top of its rotation. As you apply weight, one leg gets longer as the other leg gets shorter. The goal is to apply very similar movements to the skis.
2. From a traverse (toward the group), demonstrate pedaling against the new outside ski while extending and opening

into a wedge. Continue pedaling, with one ski getting lighter and one heavier while you ski.

3. Ask the group to try what you have just shown them; then practice together while linking a series of turns.

Ice

Very firm snow or ice also requires some adjustments to turn shape and skill application. The hard surface of the snow provides much less resistance to rotary movements, so you should expend less effort on steering to keep from over-turning the skis. Over-turning causes excessive skidding, and makes it difficult to control the shape of the turn. Because the surface is slicker, increasing the edge angles helps provide better ski–snow interaction and utilization of ski design.

For success on hard snow and ice, focus on an early and strong commitment to the new outside ski, while using active edging movements.

Applying Turn Shapes to Different Terrain and Snow Conditions

All the efforts in Level 5 at helping students match higher in the turn ultimately lead to parallel skiing—where both edges change simultaneously. By this time, many students have been guided to the point where they regularly perform parallel turn entries on many green trails. Others will be just on the verge of parallel skiing. It is important that you neither rush nor

impede this development. Encourage and praise it when you see it, and suggest it when you see they are ready. Guide them into terrain and speed situations where parallel turns are likely to occur. The consolidation of parallel turns is the curriculum for Level 6. An introduction of the parallel turn on green terrain is appropriate for the end of Level 5.

As your students gain more experience skiing in various snow conditions, they will be increasingly interested in exploring a variety of terrain and find the mountain more enjoyable. Level 5 students will want to ski much of the mountain, and what they have learned at this level sets the stage for their continued development.

Technical Aspects of Skill Development

Balancing Movements

Balancing movements are critical to good skiing at any level. Continued development and improvement of flexion and extension improves balance by reinforcing the importance of maintaining solid contact between the shin and the boot tongue. These movements encourage an active range of motion. The chances of being pushed out of balance are reduced—even in moguls and powder—because active flexion and extension helps students apply constant adjustments to balance while skiing. During the second half of the turn, flexion lowers the center of mass over the skis, which also aids

balance. Learning to change the rate of the flexion and extension helps students learn to make both shorter and longer turns. Students develop their balance further when they learn to start their turns with a smaller wedge. As they narrow the wedge, lateral stability is reduced; with the smaller wedge, students learn to refine their ability to maintain balance over this narrower platform. Introducing the pole plant aids in balance and stability because it adds a third point of contact during the edge change. By planting the pole, even with a narrow wedge opening, students increase the size of the platform. Balance and flow are enhanced as students learn to move more laterally than vertically by following the pole swing.

Rotary Movements

As students learn to vary the size and shape of their turns, they also learn to regulate the timing of rotary movements. Shorter turns require quicker, more active steering movements of the foot and leg. These turns are executed from a taller stance, which makes the skis easier to steer because there is less resistance from the edges (see edge-control movements). Conversely, slower, more patient steering movements are used to make medium turns. Although students learned to actively steer their inside leg when they learned to match and skid for the first time, they refine this inside leg steering as they learn to match earlier (see the Skier Level 4 section in this study guide). Inside leg steering is further developed and refined with garland exercises, uphill christies, and sideslipping. The movement of tipping the ski onto its edge starting with the foot (and involving the ankle, knee, and hip joints) produce an internal leg rotation (toward the midline of the body). This internal rotation becomes a passive steering movement which directs the ski.

Edge–control movements

Students are learning to refine their edging skills with more subtle adjustments. Some of these adjustments are related simply to a taller stance, which reduces the amount of edge engagement. As they steer their skis more across the hill, however, more edge angle develops. This is exactly what allows students of all levels to stand still when their skis are placed perpendicular to the fall line. To flatten the skis so that they can be steered into the new turn, active extension becomes more important.

Students also work on actively increasing edge angles with uphill christies, skating, and sideslipping. At this level, edges are changed sequentially (first one, then the other). The edge of the new outside ski is changed when the skis are opened into a wedge; the edge change is completed when the inside ski is steered to a matched relationship. Sideslipping helps to build simultaneous (both skis together and at the same time) edging movements. Focus on edging and applying pressure to the ski causes it to turn, as it did in wedge pedals. This is especially true on hard snow or ice because it offers little resis-

tance to turning the ski. The focus, therefore, is on engaging the edges to keep the skis from slipping or skidding excessively and over-turning. In deeper snow or powder, blending edging movements with rotary movements allow the ski to bend into more of an arc (because it is tipped) and the ski itself helps make the turn.

Pressure–control Movements

Students are learning more active control of pressure over their skis more actively, both along the length of the ski, and from foot to foot. Flexion increases pressure to the tongue of the boot, helping to keep even pressure on the length of the ski. The earlier match requires that pressure be transferred to the new outside ski higher in the turn, resulting in a lighter inside ski earlier in the turn. The inside ski is difficult to steer to a matched relationship if the skis are still equally weighted.

Skiing over small bumps helps students become more sensitive to where they are on their feet (over the ball or more on the heel), and is an excellent means of helping them learn to make adjustments while skiing.

As students learn to round out and finish the turns, they also begin to feel more pressure develop on the outside ski. The continued, progressive flexion helps keep the outside ski from being overloaded. As the center of mass is lowered over the outside ski, some of the pressure is absorbed (as the body is lowered toward the pull of gravity). Edge angles are increased during

the second half of the turn and pressure builds because the surface area of the ski is decreased. Pressure control through flexion is an important element in finishing the turn smoothly.

Level 5 Questions: From Wedge Christie to Beginning Parallel; Exploring Blue Runs and Varied Snow Conditions

1.   What is the advantage mentioned in the study guide of having your Level 5 students ski to a designated meeting spot during the warm–up run (rather than having them follow you in a line)?

   _____

2.   According to the study guide, when might it be safer to lead your group through the first few turns at the beginning of a Level 5 lesson?

   _____

3.   Choose the best answer:
   Which of the following skills do the majority of your beginning Level 5 students use (more than the rest) to change the shape and size of their turns?
   A.   Pressure control
   B.   Steering
   C.   Edging

4.   Circle the best choice:
   Steering more actively with both feet and legs during the initiation of a turn will create a (shorter) / (longer) turn shape.

5.   Choose the best answer:
   Having your level 5 students use a taller stance:
   A.   Helps keep their skis flatter in the snow
   B.   Makes their skis easier to steer
   C.   Should not be used for progressions involving shorter–radius turns
   D.   Should not be used for progressions involving longer–radius turns

6.   Choose one or more of the following:
   To demonstrate shorter crescent–shaped turns on fairly flat terrain during a Level 5 lesson, you should:
   A.   Begin to flex in the ankles and knees over the outside ski prior to transferring your weight to it
   B.   Begin to flex in the ankles and knees over the outside ski after transferring weight to it
   C.   Begin to flex immediately before your skis are in the fall line
   D.   Begin to flex about when your skis are in the fall line

7.   Choose one or more of the following:
   Which of the following types of shorter turns is/are most likely to be appropriate for your Level 5 students on flatter sections of the mountain:
   A.   Round, but unfinished turns
   B.   Round, finished turns
   C.   Z–shaped turns

8. Circle the best choice:

Steering slowly and patiently throughout a turn helps create (a longer, more open) / (a shorter, more closed) turn shape.

9. Circle the best choice:

(More) / (less) effort is required for medium–radius turns than for shorter–radius turns.

10. Circle the best choice:

Runs that are steeper will demand a (less) / (more) finished turn shape to keep your students from going too fast.

11. Choose one or more of the following:

To help control your speed in medium–radius turns:
A. Continue to steer as you come back across the fall line
B. Begin to steer as you come back across the fall line
C. Make a more open turn
D. Make a more finished turn

12. Choose one or more of the following:

During medium-radius turns, as the skis come across the hill, which of the following will help round out the bottom of the turn?
A. The increased edge angle which naturally develops on the outside ski
B. The increased pressure which naturally develops on the outside ski
C. Steering
D. None of the above

13. Choose the best answer:

Compared to short–radius turns, in medium–radius turns:
A. Edge angles will increase
B. Pressure will increase
C. Edge and pressure will increase

14. Choose one or more of the following:

Why is extension more important to help start a medium-radius turn than a short–radius turn?
A. It helps release the edges
B. It allows the skis to be steered more easily
C. It helps absorb pressure

15. Circle the best choice:

If you have your students shorten their turns by steering more quickly and actively (all else being equal), they would tend to (speed up) / (slow down).

16. Choose one or more of the following:
     Decreasing the amount of flexion and extension movements in your turn will help promote:
     A. An earlier matching
     B. A better weight transfer
     C. Better pressure control over the outside ski
     D. None of the above

17. Briefly describe the "counting progression" given in the study guide for encouraging your students
     to progressively extend and flex throughout their turns.

     _____

     _____

     _____

     _____

     _____

     _____

18. Fill in the blanks (with one or more words) in the following description of a Level 5 sideslipping
     demonstration:

     A. From a static position with your skis across the hill, release the skis' edges by relaxing the legs and
         rolling the ankles and knees slightly down the hill.
         As your edges release their grip in the snow, your skis will begin to _____.

     B. After your skis have slipped a few feet, _____ to engage the edges again and
         come to a stop. (Indicate what you would do with your feet, ankles, and knees)

19. True or false:
     When demonstrating a sideslip for your Level 5 students, you should hold your hands quietly
     in front of your body to promote good balance and body position.

20. Choose the best answer:
     During sideslipping, your Level 5 students should focus on feeling:
     A. The ball of the foot
     B. The heel of the foot
     C. The entire bottom of the foot

21. If your weight is forward during a sideslip, in which direction might you expect to move?

     _____

22. Fill in the blank:
Tie flexion and extension movements into sideslipping by having students _____ as they

roll their knees and ankles down the hill, and _____ as they re–engage their edges.

23. Below are some of the skills which either skating or sideslipping can help your students develop.
Write either skating or sideslipping in the space provided to the right of each skill.

A. A more active weight transfer _____

B. Simultaneous movements of the legs _____

C. Independent movements of the legs _____

24. Fill in the blank:
In order to push off from a ski when skating, the ski must be _____.

25. Circle the best choice:
For skating, emphasize tipping the leg (inward) / (outward) while flexing in the ankle.

26. Define "guided discovery."

_____

_____

27. True or false:
A smaller wedge will make it easier for Level 5 students to steer their inside leg to match the outside leg.

28. Choose the best answer:
In wedge christie turns, as students extend and steer into a small wedge:
A. The inside knee is inside the platform of the skis
B. The inside knee is outside the platform of the skis
C. Both knees are inside the platform of the skis
D. Both knees are aligned directly over the platform of the skis

29. Circle the best choice:
In order to steer the inside ski sooner, the weight has to be committed to the (inside) / (outside)
ski higher in the turn.

30. Circle the best choice:
As students steer their skis more across the hill (less) / (more) edge angle will develop.

31. The exercise described in the study guide for enhancing inside leg steering and edging movements begins with garlands and progresses to what (as a final stage of the progression)?

   _____

32. Circle the best choice:
   The study guide describes how to perform garlands by starting in a shallow traverse and then actively rolling the uphill knee and ankle into the hill while balancing on the (downhill) / (uphill) ski.

33. Choose the best answer:
   During the Level 5 garland exercise described in the study guide, you first flex and tip your inside leg into the hill and then extend. What happens to your skis when you extend?
   A. Your skis will carry you back across the hill
   B. The tails of your skis will start down the hill
   C. The tips of your skis will start down the hill

34. Choose one or more of the following:
   During the uphill christie progression described for this level, when you flex your ankles and knees slightly forward and inward, you should:
   A. Move your hips slightly downhill from your feet
   B. Keep your hips over your feet
   C. Move your hips slightly uphill of your feet

35. Choose the best answer:
   In uphill christies, what would be the result of tipping the ankles and knees only slightly into the turn (as opposed to the normal amount):
   A. The shape of the turn will become somewhat elongated
   B. The finish of the turn will become significantly shorter and tighter
   C. The shape of the turn will remain unchanged

36. The study guide suggests combining continued steering (to finish turns) with another skill to help control speed on steeper terrain. What is that skill?

   _____

37. What does the study guide suggest having your students try to imagine while skiing across the hill to get them to position their hands properly for a pole plant?

   _____

38. Choose one or more of the following:
   Students learning to plant their poles sometimes drop their inside hand after the pole plant. This:
   A. Requires an extra, less efficient movement to get ready to plant the pole for the next turn
   B. Should be encouraged
   C. Could lead to over–rotating the body
   D. None of the above

39. Circle the best choice:

To help students learn where to position their hands (in preparation for learning how to plant their poles), this study guide suggests having them traverse the hill while continuously pressing with the (heels) / (palms) of the hands to get the pole points to leave two distinct lines in the snow.

40. Choose one or more of the following:

For pole plants at this level (assume slow to moderate speeds on easy, flat, hardpacked blue terrain):
   A.   Students should plant the point of the pole in front and somewhat to the side of their boots (somewhere in the front third of the ski)
   B.   Students should plant the point of the pole to the side of their boots
   C.   Students should plant the point of the pole in front and somewhat to the side of the student's boots (somewhere in the middle third of the ski)
   D.   There should be at least a couple of feet between the pole point and the skis
   E.   There should be no more than one foot between the pole plant and the skis
   F.   Students should swing the pole by moving the wrist
   G.   Student should swing the pole by moving the upper arm

41. Circle the best choice:

When teaching your students a more dynamic pole plant, have them plant the point just (after) / (before) they match their skis.

42. What reason does the study guide give for suggesting that you have students who are learning to plant their poles use medium–radius turns?

_____

43. Some students at this level plant the wrong pole. What does the study guide suggest having your students try to imagine to correct this problem?

_____

44. The frog hunting progression for teaching students pole action has them imagine that they have a flashlight in their uphill hand. What should they imagine they will be using their downhill pole for?

_____

45. Circle the best choice:

For medium–radius turns (moderate speed, easy blue run), students should begin to swing their pole in preparation for the next turn (as they enter the fall line) / (after they have exited the fall line).

46. The study guide mentions a number of benefits a Level 5 student can gain by having a good pole plant. Name one of these:

_____

47.   Define "flow of the center of mass."

_____

_____

48.   Choose the best answer:
      To teach a more lateral movement in turns, the study guide suggests having the group imagine that there is a small rope between the point of each pole and the:
      A.   Hip
      B.   Shoulder
      C.   Waist

49.   Choose the best answer:
      The study guide also contains a static exercise for teaching students to extend more laterally. When performing this exercise, you want the skis to begin moving due to:
      A.   The edge release
      B.   The edge engagement
      C.   The momentum generated by a quick extension followed by a sudden halting of that movement
      D.   The momentum generated by a slowly initiated extension followed by a sudden halting of that movement

50.   Choose the best answer:
      Having your students try to ski runs that vary from flatter to steeper at the same pace should:
      A.   Cause them to change the shape of their turns
      B.   Have no effect on the shape of their turns
      C.   Not be tried at this level

51.   Choose the best answer:
      In small moguls, the study guide suggests having your students:
      A.   Plant the pole down the side and begin their turn between the moguls
      B.   Plant the pole and begin their turn down the side of the mogul
      C.   Plant the pole and begin their turn on the flat spot on top of the mogul
      D.   None of the above

52.   What does the study guide mention as being a disadvantage of skiing with stiff legs in bumps?

_____

53.   What reason does the study guide give for having students extend fairly slowly in small moguls?

_____

54. Select either number 1, 2, or 3 from each column:

When you ski in powder rather than on packed snow:

Column A.   Your turn shape should be:

Column B.   Resistance from the snow will be:

Column C.   The amount of effort you will need to put into your steering movements will be:

A.	B.	C.
1. Straighter	1. Less	1. Less
2. Rounder	2. More	2. More
3. The same	3. The same	3. The same

55. Circle the best choice:

In powder, good flexion and extension movements will help (reduce) / (increase) the resistance between the skis and the snow.

56. Choose the best answer:

To make up for the increased resistance from powder, you should steer

A.   Quickly

B.   Powerfully

C.   Quickly and powerfully

57. Circle the best choice:

In ice or very firm snow, the hard surface of the snow provides much (less) / (more) resistance to rotary movements, so you should expend (less) / (more) effort on steering to keep from over–turning the skis.

58. Indicate whether you would use each of the following fundamental skills "more actively," "less actively," or "the same amount" on ice as you would on hardpacked snow:

A.   Rotary _____

B.   Edge Control _____

C.   Pressure Control _____

59. Choose the best answer:

Learning to change the rate of their flexion and extension will help students:

A.   Learn to make shorter turns

B.   Learn to make longer turns

C.   Learn to make both shorter and longer turns

D.   None of the above

60. Read the following descriptions of movements and skills that were introduced or refined during the Level 5 lesson and then write the name of the fundamental skill primarily involved in the space provided. (Fundamental skills: Balance, Rotary, Edge Control, Pressure Control)

    A.   Students refine this skill when they learn to ski in a narrower wedge because a narrower wedge results in reduced lateral stability. _____

    B.   Matching the skis earlier requires that the student transfer weight to the new outside ski higher in the turn, thereby making the inside ski lighter sooner._____

    C.   Executing a shorter turn requires quicker, more active steering movements of the foot and leg._____

    D.   Use this skill to keep the skis from slipping or skidding excessively and to keep from overturning.

         _____

    E.   A taller stance reduces the amount of edge engagement. _____

    F.   By planting the pole, even with a narrow wedge opening, students increase the size of the platform.

         _____

    G.   Continued and progressive flexion helps keep the outside ski from being overloaded because as the center of mass is lowered over the outside ski, some of the force is absorbed (as the body is lowered toward the pull of gravity).

         _____

Level 5 Answers: From Wedge Christie to Beginning Parallel; Exploring Blue Runs and Varied Snow Conditions

1.   It's easier to watch them. If you have your Level 5 students ski on their own to a designated meeting spot during their warm–up run rather than following you in a line, you will find it much easier to watch them during their first few turns. Consult your trainer to determine whether it is best to use this method or to have your students follow you down the hill.

2.   When there is a lot of traffic on that part of the hill. You might want to lead your group through the first few turns at the beginning of a Level 5 lesson *to move them safely through a high traffic area.*

3.   B. The primary skill students at this level use to change the shape and size of their turns is *steering.*

4.   Shorter. Steering more actively with both feet and legs during the initiation of a turn will create a *shorter* turn shape.

5.   A & B. Using a taller stance will help keep your Level 5 students' skis flatter in the snow and will make them *easier to steer.* Students are asked to assume a taller stance for both the shorter radius turn progression and the medium–radius turn progression described in the first few pages of the Level 5 text in the study guide.

6.   B & D. When showing your Level 5 students how to make shorter, crescent–shaped turns on fairly flat terrain, you should flex over the outside ski to keep from over-edging on this flatter terrain. As you begin to flex (roughly when your skis are in the fall line), you should have completed transferring your weight to the new outside ski. You will probably match the inside ski at about the same time.

7.   A. Short, round, but unfinished turns result in the your being able to maintain your speed, while still being in control. The fact that this type of turn allows the skis to continue gliding well on the snow makes it appropriate for flatter sections of any mountain.

8.   A longer, more open. Steering slowly and patiently throughout a turn helps create a *longer, more open* turn shape.

9.   Less. *Less* effort is required for medium–radius turns because there is more time to turn the skis

10. More. Runs that are steeper will demand a *more* finished turn shape to keep your students from going too fast.

11. A & D. While having your students practice medium-radius turns, ask them to be aware of the sensation of slowing down as they come back across the fall line. Be sure that each member of your group understands that this continued steering is what controls speed. Completing their turns will also help control their speed.

12. A, B, & C. During medius–radius turns, as the skis come across the hill, more edge angle and pressure will naturally develop on the outside/downhill ski, which will combine with steering to help round out the bottom of the turn.

13. C. Edge and pressure increase in a medium–radius turn. Extension becomes more important to help start the next turn because it helps release the edges and allows your students to steer their skis more easily. For this reason, be sure to encourage the members of your group to make a good extension movement as they open their skis into a wedge.

14. A & B. In medium–radius turns (as compared to shorter-radius turns), extension becomes more important to help start the next turn because it helps release the edges and allows students to steer their skis more easily.

15. Slow down. If you have your students shorten their turns by steering more quickly and actively, they should *slow down* (all else being equal).

16. D. None of the above. Slightly *more* dynamic flexion and extension movements help promote an earlier matching and better weight transfer and pressure control over the outside ski.

17. The following progression can help your students realize that they should extend gradually and continuously almost to the fall line and flex gradually and continuously throughout the second half of their turns.
    Demonstrate, then have your students try to make a round, finished medium turn while counting to three while extending, and to three again while flexing, as follows:
    On 1, start to extend.
    On 2, after having initiated the turn, continue to rise.
    On 3, when you are almost in the fall line, come to the peak of your extension.
    Repeat the three–count while flexing and finishing the turn.
    You should count out loud, but should consider having your students count to themselves as they will probably feel less self–conscious that way.

18. Slip laterally. Tip your feet, ankles, and knees back into the hill.
    To sideslip:
    A. From a static position with your skis across the hill, release the skis' edges by relaxing the legs and rolling the ankles and knees slightly down the hill.
        As your edges release their grip in the snow, your skis will begin to *slip laterally*.
    B. After your skis have slipped a few feet, *tip your feet, ankles, and knees back into the hill gradually* to engage the edges again and come to a stop.

19. True. When demonstrating a sideslip for your Level 5 students, you should hold your hands quietly in front of your body to promote good balance and body position.

20. C. To keep centered while sideslipping, your Level 5 students should focus on feeling the whole bottom of the foot inside the ski boot.

21. Diagonally forward. If your weight is forward during a sideslip, you can expect your skis to move diagonally forward.

22. Extend, flex. Tie flexion and extension movements into sideslipping by having them *extend* as they roll their knees and ankles down the hill, and *flex* as they re-engage their edges.

23. A. Skating, B. Sideslipping, C. Skating.
     As these students begin to explore a broader spectrum of runs on the mountain, skating will make them *more mobile, and can be used to help develop a more active weight transfer and independent movements of the legs.* Sideslipping will develop the *simultaneous (same time, same direction) use of both feet, ankles, and legs.* These simultaneous movements are an important building block for working toward parallel turns.

24. Edged. In order to push off from a ski when skating, it must be *edged.* Be sure to actively extend while pushing off from that ski.

25. Inward. For skating, emphasize tipping the leg *inward* to edge the ski while flexing in the ankle.

26. In guided discovery you lead your students through a series of steps or exercises so that they discover outcomes on their own.
     The study guide utilizes this technique when it suggests having your students narrow their wedges and increase their speed to force them to commit themselves to the outside ski higher in the turn to maintain balance and control. (Early weight transfer)

27. True. In making a smaller wedge, the inside leg is in a better position to be steered to a matching relationship.

28. C. As your students extend and steer into a small wedge when they make a wedge–christie turn, both knees will be inside the platform of the skis. By rotating the inside foot and knee further toward the center of the turn, the inside ski will pivot easily on the snow. This is especially true if the inside ski is fairly light (due to a shift of most of the weight to the outside ski).

29. Outside. In order to steer the inside ski sooner, the weight has to be committed to the *outside* ski higher in the turn.

30. More. As students steer their skis more across the hill *more* edge angle will develop.

31. A series of wedge–christie turns. The exercise described in the study guide for enhancing inside leg steering and edging movements begins with garlands and ends with *a series of wedge–christie turns.*

32. Downhill. To demonstrate the garland exercise, begin in a shallow traverse (toward the group) and then actively roll the inside knee and ankle into the hill while maintaining pressure and balancing on the outside or downhill ski.

33. C. Each time you extend in the garland exercise described in the study guide, your ski tips will start down the hill. Each time you flex and tip your inside leg, your tips will stop drifting down the hill and will begin to carry you back across the hill.

34. B. When you flex your ankles and knees slightly forward and inward to tip the skis onto their edges in an uphill christie, the design of the ski will cause the skis to climb back up into the hill in a shallow turn. The hips should remain over the feet and the hands should be comfortably up and in front of the body.

35. A. During an uphill christie, tipping your ankles and knees very slightly into the turn will cause the turn to become somewhat elongated. (Tipping the knees and ankles more aggressively toward the inside of the turn will cause the finish of an uphill christie to become significantly shorter and tighter).

36. Active edging. When active edging is combined with continued steering of the feet and skis, the design of the skis helps to finish the turn back across the fall line, which controls speed.

37. That they are carrying a tray with cups of water on it. To help your students position their hands properly for a pole plant, it may be helpful to ask them to imagine that they are carrying a tray with cups of water on it. Tipping the tray to either side or downward will spill the water.

38. A & C. Dropping the inside hand can lead to *over-rotating your body during a turn.* Even if over–rotation is not a result, dropping the hand after the pole plant will require an extra, less efficient movement to prepare the pole for the next turn.
    The study guide suggests emphasizing the idea of using only the wrist to swing the pole, and also reminding your students of the tray with water glasses on it: they should try to hold their hands quiet to avoid spilling the water.

39. Heels. To help students learn how to position their hands (in preparation for learning how to plant their poles), the study guide suggests having them traverse the hill while continuously pressing with the *heels* of the hands to get the pole points to leave two distinct lines in the snow.

40. A & D & F. For pole plants at this level (at normal speeds), the point of the pole should be planted *in front and somewhat to the side of the student's boots (somewhere in the front third of the ski).*
    If students plant the pole too close to their skis, they will be forced to ski past the pole point before starting to turn. Therefore, *there should be at least a couple of feet between the pole point and the skis.*
    The student should swing the pole forward by *moving the wrist* without changing the relationship of the hand or arm. They should move the wrist so that the thumb moves toward them, and the heel of the hand moves away from them.

41. Before. When teaching your students a more dynamic pole plant, have them plant the point just *before* they match their skis so that it becomes a cue to match. The poles should be planted in conjunction with the edge change because it is the least stable part of the turn. In this case, matching the skis represents the edge change.

42. It gives them *time to concentrate* on their poles without having to rush into the next turn. Students who are learning to plant poles should probably make medium–radius turns because this type of turn gives them time to concentrate on their poles without having to rush into the next turn.

43. That each pole is a turn signal. One possible way to help students who plant the wrong pole is to have them think of each pole as being a turn signal, with the right pole signaling a right turn, and the left, a left turn.

44. To touch the frog. In the frog–hunting progression, students use the ski pole in their downhill hand to *catch the frog*. They swing the downhill pole forward so that they are ready to touch the frog with it while shining the light on it (with the uphill hand). As soon as they touch the frog, they make a turn. They then have to imagine that the light has switched hands. As they approach the next turn ("frog"), they should touch the frog with the new downhill pole and turn again.

45. As they enter the fall line. In medium–radius turns, students should begin to swing their pole *as they enter the fall line*, letting the movement last until the end of the turn, so that the insertion of the tip of the pole corresponds with the initiation of the next turn.

46. There are many benefits to a good pole plant. A few mentioned in the study guide are:
    • Better rhythm and timing
    • Can be an effective cue for directing extension movements more down the hill and toward the center of the next turn
    • Can be a cue to match the skis
    • Better stability (when changing edges)
    • An aid to balance in all situations, but especially on steeper terrain, bumps, and powder

47. The movement of the student's body from one turn to the next is commonly referred to as a *flow of the center of mass*.

48. A. To teach a more lateral movement in turns, ask your group to imagine that there is a small rope between the point of each pole and the *adjacent hip*. The rope is long enough for them to swing the pole without interference, but short enough that as they swing the pole, the rope pulls their hip in the same direction. As they swing the pole, they should extend up, forward, and across the skis. Their hip should move enough for their skis to flatten and begin to slip. Because they have moved forward as well, their ski tips should begin down the hill and toward the top of a new turn.

49. A. It important to extend slowly when performing the static exercise for directing your extension and releasing the edges because you want the skis to begin moving due to the edge release, not because of the momentum generated by a quick extension, followed by a sudden halting of that movement.

50. A. Having your students try to ski runs that vary from flatter to steeper at the same pace is one way to force them to change the shape of their turns

51. C. The study guide suggests having students plant their poles on the flat spot at the top of small moguls to help them identify the correct place to initiate their turn. (This will aid their balance, also.) Beginning their turn on that spot will also make it easier to steer into the new turn.

52. Being pushed out of balance. Skiing with the legs too stiff in bumps, particularly, can lead to being *pushed out of balance*.

53. To reduce the chance of losing ski-snow contact. Students should extend fairly slowly in small moguls *to reduce the chance of losing ski-snow contact* as they ski over the top of the bump. They should also flex fairly gradually and progressively. This will promote good balance during the finish of the turn.

54. 1, 2, 2.
Column A-1. Although a *straighter* turn shape (one that is closer to the fall line) is an accelerating turn on groomed terrain, in powder, it is the turn shape that will provide enough glide to make it easier to initiate the new turn.

Column B-2. Deeper snow creates *more* resistance than packed snow, which means you will go more slowly in powder than on groomed snow. (A round, finished turn will cause you to slow down too much and make it difficult to start the new turn.)

Column C-2. Because of the increased resistance your students will need to put *more effort* into their steering movements. Explain that the steering movements will require more power, but should still be patiently executed.

55. Reduce. In powder, good flexion and extension movements will help *reduce* the resistance between the skis and the snow, and will help provide the necessary increase in muscular power necessary to steer your skis in powder.

56. B. Students often mistake quick steering for powerful steering. Steering quickly will cause the skis to get caught in the powder, and will interrupt balance. Emphasize progressive flexion and extension movements, and steering during the range of motion (the flexion and extension movements).

57. Less, less. In very firm snow or ice, the hard surface of the snow provides much *less* resistance to rotary movements, so you should expend *less* effort on steering to keep from over-turning the skis. Over turning will cause excessive skidding, and will make it difficult to control the shape of the turn.

58. A. Less actively, B. More actively, C. More actively.
You should use edge and pressure-control movements more actively on very firm snow or ice to compensate for the reduced rotary movement. Because the surface is slicker, increasing the edge angles will help provide better ski–snow interaction and utilization of ski design.
 Focusing on an earlier and stronger commitment to the new outside ski and using active edging movements will lead to success on hard snow and ice.

59. C. Learning to change the rate of the flexion and extension will help students learn to make both shorter and longer turns.

60. A. Balance. Students develop their balance further when they learn to start their turns with a smaller wedge. As they narrow their wedge, lateral stability is reduced; with the smaller wedge, students learn to refine their ability to maintain balance over this narrower platform.
B. Pressure–control movements: Matching the skis earlier requires that the student transfer pressure to the new outside ski higher in the turn, thereby making the inside ski lighter sooner.
C. Rotary movements: Executing a shorter turn requires quicker, more active steering movements of the foot and leg. These turns are executed from a taller stance, which makes the skis easier to steer because there is less resistance from the edges.
D. Edge–control movements: Engage the edges to keep the skis from slipping or skidding excessively and over-turning. In deeper snow or powder, blending edging movements with rotary movements will allow the ski to bend into more of an arc (because it is tipped over) and the ski itself will help make the turn.

E. Edge–control movements: Students are learning to refine their edging skills with more subtle adjustments. Some of these adjustments are related simply to a taller stance, which reduces the amount of edge engagement.

F. Balance. Introducing the pole plant aids in balance and stability because it adds a third point of contact during the edge change. By planting the pole, even with a narrow wedge opening, students increase the size of the platform.

G. Pressure–control movements: Continued and progressive flexion helps keep the outside ski from being overloaded because as the center of mass is lowered over the outside ski, some of the pressure is absorbed (as the body is lowered toward the pull of gravity).

Notes:

Skier Level 6

Parallel Turns

View this information not as a lesson plan for one day of lessons, but a collection of information that you can use to customize lessons for your students. If you need more help designing individual lesson plans, consult your ski school trainer—and be creative.

Lesson Outcome

Students learn to initiate their turns with their skis parallel.

Note: The difference in mechanics between a wedge (or stem) christie and a parallel turn is described to help give a better understanding of how to teach parallel turn entries.

Introduction to Parallel Turn Initiation

Most students find this lesson exciting because they are anxious to learn parallel skiing. How do you know when they're ready? When they can successfully link wedge (or stem) christie turns on easier blue runs in most snow conditions, they are ready. Many of these students will already be able to make rudimentary parallel turns on green slopes, as well as advanced wedge christies on blue slopes. Students often feel comfortable with their wedge–christie turns because these turns provide them with the security of being able to keep their weight over the old outside ski when they start a new turn. In contrast, in a parallel

turn, they are asked to transfer weight to the new outside ski before they start the turn. While it is possible to make parallel turns without an active and relatively early weight transfer, such a weight transfer will actually help them learn to make parallel turns and is fundamental to good skiing. Photo 10 depicts a parallel turn.

Terrain

Select moderate terrain (green or very easy blue) that is comfortable for every member of your class and is not too crowded. The slope should be well groomed and gentle enough for them to try new and un-familiar movements without fear of losing control.

Class Arrangement and Handling

The best format is probably a huddle or small circular formation as opposed to a lineup. This format will allow everyone to see demonstrations clearly in a non–intimidating atmosphere.

Foot–to–Foot Movements That Establish Early Weight Transfer

Start with your group at the edge of the trail.

1. Describe the movements and sensations of actively moving your weight from one ski to the other while you demonstrate movements statically. Encourage the students to make one ski heavy while they make

Photo 10. Parallel Turn

A

B

C

the other ski light—then make the light ski heavy and the heavy one light. You accomplish this by pressing down on the foot you wish to weight. It may be helpful to actually lift the light ski off the snow during the static exercise.

2. Watch each member of the group to be sure that they understand the movements. If they are not executing the weight shift, try to explain the idea in different words. Also, watch to make sure that they are not moving their hips and shoulders from side to side as while shifting weight from foot to foot. The transfer should come from movements of the legs and feet underneath a quiet upper body.

3. When the students show that they can shift weight from foot to foot statically, have them put the same movements into action while sliding on the snow. If the run is very flat, you can ski more or less in the fall line; if not, traverse across the hill while making your skis alternately heavy and light. Again, it may be helpful to actually lift the light ski slightly during the exercise, but explain that the goal is to have both skis on the snow while turning even though they are not equally weighted.

4. Have students repeat this exercise in both directions, and then practice it enough to develop comfort with the required movements. Be careful, though, not to ask them to practice so long that they become bored with the exercise. Two traverses

while practicing will probably be sufficient.

Incorporating Flexion and Extension

During the exercise, encourage your group to extend off of the newly weighted ski as they lift the other foot and ski slightly. When they transfer back to the downhill ski, suggest that they flex in the ankles and knees a bit. Flexion and extension movements facilitate weight transfer and help anchor the idea that flexion and extension are an integral part of skiing!

Note: While having your students practice the weight transfer in a traverse, you must be especially aware of the flow of traffic on the slope. Ideally, find a trail in a low traffic area. However, if the trail is busier, wait for a break in the flow of traffic and then call your group across the slope in pairs, with one student higher up the hill than the other. The students can then practice the weight transfer simultaneously without interfering with each other. You may continue using this form of class handling throughout this segment of the lesson.

Skating

If your group seems skilled, or if the terrain is quite flat, you can introduce and/or develop skating. Skating helps develop more active weight transfer, independent leg movement, and edge–control movements, and it helps to anchor flexion and extension. If the terrain is flat, teach the following progres-

sion in or near the fall line. If the terrain has a bit more pitch, teach the progression primarily across the hill.

Start from a static position at the side of the trail.

1. Flex over the downhill ski.
2. Describe and demonstrate extension that is directed forward and across that ski while transferring weight to the uphill ski. Execute this movement by pushing off of the downhill ski while propelling your body forward. In order to push from the ski, it must be edged.
3. As weight is transferred to the uphill ski, begin to flex in that ankle and knee while rolling that ski onto its edge.
   Emphasize light pressure on the tongue of the boot to stay centered.
4. Repeat the movements as you push back to the downhill ski.
5. Demonstrate the same movements while skiing toward the group.
6. Repeat the demonstration, this time moving away from the group.
7. Skate from foot to foot at least two or three times without stopping.
8. Give your students the opportunity to try skating on their own, then have them practice together. The most common difficulties for students result from a lack of edge engagement, or from standing too tall, without sufficient flex in the ankle. Emphasize tipping the leg to edge the ski during ankle flexion.

Combining Pole Use with Weight Transfer

Your demonstration should include a pole plant if at least some members of your group are using a pole plant when they turn. For now, try not to emphasize pole use too much because it may detract from students' ability to focus on the newer elements you are teaching. Each time you transfer weight to the uphill ski, swing the pole tip; plant the downhill pole as you extend.

If your students need to learn to plant their poles, you must decide whether to change the focus of your lesson or to proceed for now without the pole plant. To introduce both the pole plant and the parallel initiation concurrently would surely overwhelm students! (For more information on introducing pole usage, see the Level 5 section of this study guide).

Improving Outside Leg Steering

The next step is to review or teach independent steering of the new outside leg, foot, and ski. Again, group your students at the edge of a trail.

1. Show them how easy it is to steer the foot and ski when they lift them off the snow.
2. Describe how the movement of twisting the foot from side to side can be accomplished simply by pointing the toes downhill and then back toward the top of the trail.
3. Explain that when standing with your foot off the snow at the side of a run, there is no resistance to turning the ski. When skiing, though, steering the ski requires a stronger twisting movement including the foot, ankle, and knee, to actively guide the ski.
4. Repeat this movement with the other foot, ankle, and knee.
5. Demonstrate a turn in which you emphasize first the weight transfer with extension and then active steering of the new ski involving the foot, ankle, and ultimately the whole leg .

To give your students the best view, consider hiking up the hill so that you can demonstrate a turn going toward them. Use a pole plant, if appropriate. You should ski this turn to a stop.
6. Answer any questions your students may have.
7. Show them another turn going away from them. Multiple views and perspectives help them see the maneuver.

Note: The students in your group will quickly get a feeling for starting to turn their skis from their feet first, then involving the rest of the leg for more power. This is important because they begin to learn fine motor control: the ability to refine and control movements with different parts of their bodies.

One–at–a–Time versus Task Style

Now that your students are ready to try a turn with earlier weight transfer and active steering of the new ski, you must decide how you will orchestrate their movements on the hill. Consider using either the one–at–a–time or the task teaching styles (See Table 2).

How you move the group is up to you; experiment with different ways of moving the group, and with a variety of teaching styles to determine what seems to work best for you and your students.

Adding Active Inside Leg Steering

With practice, feedback, and encouragement, most students quickly succeed in transferring weight to the new ski before using the foot and leg to guide that ski into the new turn. Emphasizing flexion and extension aids in balance and make steering the new ski easier. Even when they accurately execute those movements, some students may still experience a slight wedge opening at turn initiation. This is usually a result of inside leg inactivity. Now is the time to focus on steering the inside leg more actively.

Describe the sensation of twisting or steering with the outside foot: there is a sensation of pressure on the inner (big toe) side of the ball of the foot where it touches the inside of the ski boot. To steer the inside ski, create similar pressure on the outer (little toe) side of the ball of the foot inside the ski boot. Active inside leg steering is evident in photo 11. With careful involvement of the inside leg, the inside ski turns the same amount and at the same time as the outside ski, even though the outside ski carries almost all of the weight.

Table 2

One-at-a-time versus Task Style			
Teaching Style	Description	Pros	Cons
One–at–a–time (Command)	You tell each student when to come down the hill.	Enables you to check each individual's understanding. Gives you a chance to provide feedback for each student.	The group has to stand longer in one place on the hill Can place unnecessary pressure on some people because they (correctly) feel that everyone is watching them.
Task	You choose a designated point somewhere farther down the trail where everyone will regroup.	Gives everyone the chance to try combining the movements.	You have to watch everyone for a few turns each and remember how well each person executed the task so that you can provide feedback when you regroup.

If that is too refined for your students, have them twist the inside foot while pointing the inside knee in the desired direction. The increased power of using the whole leg makes the inside ski turn even more easily.

Demonstrate and then have your students try this exercise to help anchor the sensation of inside foot steering.

1. While standing statically on relatively flat terrain with your skis perpendicular to the fall line, place the tip of the downhill ski pole in the snow next to the downhill ski (just in front of the toe piece).

2. Place the tip of the uphill pole in the snow so that both poles can be used for balance.

3. Lift the downhill ski a few inches off the snow.

4. Twist the downhill foot by pressing the inner (little toe) side of the ball of the downhill foot against the shell of the ski boot. Because the pole is in the way, you will feel added resistance to twisting the ski. This resistance highlights the sensation of actively turning the inside foot.

5. To increase power for this inside leg and foot steering, tip the downhill knee down the hill as well. When you tip your knee and twist your foot at the same time, you can exert more power against your ski pole.

6. If you want even more resistance, you can place your uphill pole between the tails of your skis.

7. Repeat the same process on the other side. After your students are familiar with the sensations of inside leg steering, have them link a series of turns together while practicing steering the inside ski the same amount and at the same time as the outside ski.

For this part of the lesson, short skiing segments (8–15 turns) are probably best. The reasons for this are twofold: 1) you can keep the group moving, and 2) you can provide feedback while helping students anchor the appropriate movements. If the skiing segments are too long, incorrect movements may be reinforced. If the segments are too short, though, there is not enough repetition of the new movements.

Checking for understanding during this part of the lesson is probably most effectively done by watching the students' performance. Asking questions of your students is another means of checking for understanding, but may be more appropriate as a follow–up after you have provided feedback and/or corrections. Asking what each student will concentrate on during the next segment helps focus their efforts after your feedback. By watching them ski, you can assess their performance and efforts. When learning something new, mistakes are inevitable— encourage and reward both their efforts and their success.

Once individual members of your group can ski the correct movements in the right combination, it is time for practice. Allow longer skiing segments with less feedback. Although you don't provide as much feedback, it does not mean you are inattentive. Keep an eye on each individual so that you can provide corrections, as needed. This is a good time to remind them of flexion and extension movements and have them practice those movements in conjunction with weight transfer and steering both skis. Students may forget about vertical motion when focusing on the relatively new movements presented in the lesson, so

Photo 11. Inside Leg Steering

don't hesitate to reinforce it. Each person learns at his or her own rate—try to avoid overload.

Note: You may also want to vary the terrain by skiing different runs, but be careful not to increase the challenge too much. It is more important to anchor the movements during this lesson than it is to try to apply these new movements to steeper runs or different snow conditions. Those challenges are presented in subsequent lessons.

Small Group versus Task Style

In this part of the lesson, experiment with different styles of class handling. You may want to use the small group style to allow your students to interact and ski in a structured, yet relaxed setting. This style allows you to work with a few people at a time while keeping everyone moving and focused. If you choose to use this style, be

aware of the entire class even though you are only working with two or three students at the moment. After part of a run, rotate to another group so that after one or two runs you have worked with each of the small groups.

Task style teaching is also very effective at this stage of the lesson. Give each individual a personal focus (relative to their personal needs), then choose and identify a place to regroup (such as a bend or a flat spot in a trail). Set up the class so that after the first person has skied one or two turns, the next member of the group starts skiing, and so on. Mix up the order on each subsequent segment so that the same person is not always first or last.

Introducing Lateral Movements During Extension

After you have provided a couple of runs to anchor what you have taught, introduce the idea of extending to make the body move down the hill and toward the new turn (so–called "lateral extension"), rather than vertically and away from the new turn. Extension at turn initiation can be seen in photo 12. Moving the body more down the hill may be intimidating. To help reduce anxiety, introduce lateral movements after your group can already make parallel turns. Since these students know that their skis will turn when they transfer weight and steer both feet, they realize—after only a few turns to practice and experience the movement—that it becomes even easier to initiate a turn using a lateral extension (i.e., extending by moving their hips slightly forward and across the skis).

Photo 12. Extension at Turn Initiation

Extending toward a Bull's Eye

With your group again arranged in a relatively small circle out of the main flow of traffic, describe and statically demonstrate the movement you wish them to achieve.

1. Draw a bull's eye in the snow. This represents the center of the turn.
2. Place the downhill ski pole in the snow to support the body and aid in balance: roughly in line with the toe piece, but far enough downhill to use as a brace.
3. While leaning on that pole, lift the downhill foot and ski a few inches off the snow, without beginning to extend.
4. With the pole in the snow and legs flexed, lift the downhill ski. Now, extend your uphill leg. More than likely, the extension will direct your center of mass toward the center of the turn. This early change of support foot helps re–direct your extension toward an imaginary target just down the hill.
5. Extend toward the bull's eye. As you begin to extend, use the whole leg to push your hips toward the bull's eye while gradually twisting the new outside ski. The edge releases and the ski starts down the hill. Extending in this new direction helps release the edges from the previous turn as the skis flatten. When the edges are released, steering becomes quite easy.
6. Once the outside ski begins to turn and slide, simply step back onto the other ski to stop.

As you can imagine, this will require a fair degree of faith from your group. Explain to them that if they can get the ski to start turning from a standstill, if will even easier to get it turning while they are moving.

Now let them practice a few turns with this focus. More than likely, each member of your group will agree that using a lateral movement to release the skis' edges helps them to start a parallel turn. Using the pole swing as a cue to start extending toward the new turn is also helpful. Then, practice skating on relatively flat terrain to refine and anchor the sensations of lateral movement.

Note: As stated before, an active and early weight transfer, although not absolutely necessary, helps with parallel turn initiation. If the preceding progression does not work well for a particular group, introduce a parallel turn with equal weight on both feet. Using the terrain and/or very active flexion and extension movements will facilitate the unweighting and edge release of the skis and will make it possible to initiate a parallel turn. The main focus of this progression is on actively steering the inside leg.

Simultaneous Steering: Hockey Slides

1. Review the use of hockey slides starting from a shallow traverse and gradually working deeper into the fall line. Hockey slides will help develop both the understanding of and ability to use simultaneous leg rotation (steering).
2. Repeat the hockey slides in both directions. Emphasize how the inside leg must mirror the activity of the outside leg to get both skis to pivot and turn at the same time. Also, be sure to demonstrate and encourage active flexion and extension.
3. Slow the rate of twisting the feet so that it lasts longer and coincides with progressive flexion.

Simultaneous Steering: Cowboy Turns

Now use the simultaneous steering from the hockey slides to introduce cowboy turns.

1. Describe the bowlegged appearance of a cowboy's legs. Explain that the goal is to make your legs look bowlegged as you start the turn by actively tipping your inside knee down the hill.
2. Ski toward your group, sliding across the hill with your weight distributed equally over both feet.
3. Ask the group to focus on what you do with the inside knee during the turn.
4. As you extend, aggressively tip your inside knee toward the intended turn while twisting both feet. This will steer both skis toward the next turn without needing a wedge. The vertical extension helps flatten the skis and release the edges, making them easier to steer.
5. Repeat the demonstration in one turn going away from the group.
6. Have your group try the exercise one at a time, first in one direction, then the other.
7. When everyone has successfully made a cowboy turn, have them link a series of these turns together in a practice segment. Continue to emphasize active flexion and extension.

Sometimes, even after you've introduced your students to hockey slides and cowboy turns, they still have difficulty with simultaneous steering—resulting in a persistent wedge during turn initiation (although it may be fairly small). The root of the problem may be the shape of the turn. If the initiation is rushed, or the turn itself too small, students may feel that the only way they can make this turn is to make a wedge as they start the turn. Develop more open, medium–sized turns by teaching patience turns.

Patience Turns

1. Describe the sensation of "relaxing tall" (extending) on both feet after the preceding turn. Instead of an active movement to start the next turn, describe a slow, passive turn entry where the ski tips gradually seek the fall line. In other words, the tips of the skis start to go down the hill and toward the new turn.
2. Demonstrate this while skiing toward your group. Choose terrain that is not intimidating for them.
3. Have the students practice this exercise. At first, ask them only

to start one turn; after the skis have begun to glide toward the fall line, they can either continue to turn while adding active flexion, tipping their ankles and knees back into the hill and steering across the slope to stop.

4. If they are comfortable making a complete turn, you can have them begin to link turns using a patience turn initiation. If not, you can work the exercise into a garland format.

  If you choose to use garlands, select terrain carefully (ideally, on a less busy trail). Gradually work the garlands deeper and deeper into the fall line until it is easier to continue the turn than to ski back across the hill.

5. Once the group can link patience turns, begin to develop more active steering movements as suggested above.

Note: If some students continue to open their skis into a slight wedge to start the turn after trying both of these options, give them more mileage and encouragement. They will probably eliminate the wedge with more practice. If not, the problem is probably either that the terrain is a little too steep, or that they need more development and practice with inside leg steering. Watch them execution carefully to determine the root of the problem.

Teaching Parallel Turns in Bumpy Conditions

Sometimes, teaching on perfectly groomed snow is impossible. Even if the weather has not changed the snow, skier traffic can—often within the course of the same day. Trying to teach an exercise that requires a run that is groomed to the point of being flat and without bumps or ripples of any kind will frustrate both you and your guests if you cannot find such a run.

  Modifying the same exercises that you taught in the previous progression to make them a little easier (i.e., introducing the exercises on terrain that is flatter than you might otherwise use) can be quite beneficial. Your students' balance will improve as they learn about terrain variation, and their visual skills will also improve by learning what to look for (i.e., snow texture). Anything you can do to help students learn to comfortably deal with a variety of snow conditions will enhance their enjoyment of the sport.

Pivoting Statically while on a Bump

When small bumps or clumps of snow are the norm, use them to an advantage by teaching students how to initiate a parallel turn on top of them.

Find a bump (or series of bumps) near the edge of a run.

1. Stand on top of the bump so that only the part of your skis that is right under your feet is in contact with the snow.
2. Demonstrating flexed knees and ankles and placing poles out to the sides for balance, twist your feet from side to side. Allow the upper body to twist opposite the feet as you twist the feet back and forth.
3. Explain that because so little of the ski is in contact with the snow, it is easy to get the skis to pivot on top of the bump.
4. Have each student stand on top of a small bump so that they, too, can experience this ease of steering. The hips and upper body should remain aligned over the feet to help keep the skis relatively flat on the snow. Encourage students to pivot their skis by creating pressure against the inside of their ski boots with the balls of their feet. Have them concentrate on pressure on the inner side of the ball of the uphill foot and the outer side of the ball of the downhill foot. This helps ski tips travel in the same direction.
5. Have students repeat this movement in the opposite direction, pivoting their skis back and forth to ground the sensation of these movements.

If you describe bumps as opportunities for turns, you can point out how many places there are to turn as you survey the slope as a group. When everyone can pivot on top of a bump while standing still, you're ready to make a turn.

Hockey Slides in the Bumps

Use hockey slides at this point to help your students become more comfortable with pivoting and skidding in the bumps.

1. From a static position on top of

a bump, demonstrate how to twist your feet down the hill as you push forward with your arms and poles. As your skis begin to slide and turn, you slip forward and down the back side of the small mogul.

2. Describe how to continue to twist both feet and skis while sliding, and point out that the starting point (the top of a bump) makes it fairly easy to start a parallel turn.

3. Encourage students to maintain some forward pressure on the boot tongue to help keep the students centered as they slide off the bump (the skis will tend to accelerate slightly as they slide down the back of the bump).

4. Ask your students (by name), one at a time, to try what you have just shown them for one turn. This will help avoid the chance of interference from one another.

5. You may need to have your students repeat this a couple of times so that everyone begins to feel more comfortable with it. The advantage of having your students start each turn from a stand-still—or at least a very slow speed—is that you can control where they start the next turn. (This will help them understand where and when to start turning.) This portion of the presentation will probably only take about five minutes.

6. Once students can execute a hockey slide from the top of a bump, have them link a series of hockey slides together into turns. Students should start each turn

with a pivot from the top of a bump, then skid their skis down the back of the bump. After they have practiced more and have become comfortable, they are able to reduce the amount of skidding in each turn.

Using Poles in the Bumps

Good pole use is helpful to students learning to ski in moguls for the first time. If your students don't already plant their poles, refer to the Level 5 pole plant progressions in this study guide. If your students already know how to plant their poles, you will only need to help them with the timing. Emphasize good hand position during skiing.

1. Show them how to begin to swing the new pole as they initiate a turn on the top of a bump. Swinging the pole fairly early helps draw their bodies forward and down the hill as they begin to turn, and leaves the pole in a ready position so that they can plant it as they ski up on top of the next mogul. Although the reduced ski-snow contact (on top of the bump) makes the skis easy to steer, it also reduces the platform. Adding the pole plant at that point improves balance and gives a sense of security by adding another point of contact during an otherwise unstable period of turn initiation.

2. As they steer their skis to start the new turn, show them how to leave the pole tip in place until they have skied past it.

3. Once past the pole tip, simply have them hinge at the wrist, rather than dropping the inside hand.

Improving Turn Shape in the Bumps

Have your students put what they have learned into action by following you through a few turns, initiating each one on top of a small bump. For now, it is probably best to have them follow you in a line so that you are choosing where to ski. Demonstrate a round, open turn shape. This allows plenty of time and room for individuals to focus on the turn initiation without having to worry immediately about the next turn. Traverse a couple of bumps, if necessary, so that your students can recover balance.

Timing exactly where to start twisting or pivoting on the bump may be challenging for students at first. Help them overcome this hurdle by allowing them to watch their feet and skis as they come to the top of the bump. As a visual cue, tell them to start steering their skis down the hill as soon as they see the toe piece of the binding reach the crest of the bump. As they get a sense for this timing, encourage them to rely less on watching the skis, and to substitute feeling the bump with the soles of their feet instead. Reinforce the concept of pressing slightly into the boot tongues to help keep centered.

A practice segment is now in order. Specify a point down the trail to regroup and let them practice on their own.

Shortening the Radius of the Turn and Enhancing Rhythm in the Bumps

As your students become more comfortable, gradually reduce the space between turns to create a better sense of rhythm. For the time being, keep the lesson on terrain that is well within the students' comfort range to avoid intimidation. An easy blue run is perfect for this, even if your students are capable of skiing more difficult blue runs in smoother snow. Begin to explore turn shapes and sizes by varying the amount of effort used to start the turn.

Up to this point, the turn entry has been somewhat passive, allowing students to learn and practice basic mechanics. Reinforce these mechanics by increasing the level of effort (or "twist") used to start the turn. Simply ask your group to make a series of turns where they steer their feet and skis more aggressively while cresting the bump. This activity leads to a shorter turn, especially if the same level of effort is applied throughout. A shorter turn will be helpful because the students are ready to start the next turn sooner. Allow plenty of practice time at this stage because quicker turns may create some challenges to balance.

Hockey Slide Progression in Bumps

To further develop the timing and movements of shorter turns, have the group practice some hockey slides in the small bumps.

1. Lead your group through a series of turns where they twist or pivot their skis quickly and powerfully on the top of a bump, then allow the skis to slip sideways down the back side of the same bump.

    Active extension in the knees and ankles helps start the turn; progressive flexion enhances balance while the skis are skidding or slipping sideways. The bumps on suitable terrain will probably be so spread out that the students have to slide forward and/or diagonally to get to the next bump.

2. Once they have maneuvered themselves to the next bump (by pushing with their poles if necessary), have them repeat the pivoting and slipping in the opposite direction.

3. Have them link these quick, short turns together into a series of 8-12 turns.

    Depending on the group, more practice may be necessary: gauge the amount of practice time by how quickly the members of the group become comfortable with the task.

4. To anchor their ability to vary turn shapes and sizes, lead the group through a series of turns where you go progressively from open, passive turns to aggressive, quicker turns and back again.

Progression for Increased Edging

So far, you and your group have been focusing on skidded turns on reasonably flat skis. Now it's time to incorporate more active edging skills. The goal is to shape the second half of the turn with a blend of rotary and edge control skills, relying on ski design to create the turn.

1. From a static position, facing across the hill, review how to use the ankles, knees, and upper leg to tip the skis on edge.

2. Show the group how rolling the ankles and knees into the hill brings the skis up onto their edges, while rolling them the other way reduces the edge angles, making the skis easier to steer.

3. Have the students practice rolling their legs into the hill while flexing at the knees and ankles, then slightly away from the hill while extending.

4. Have them repeat the exercise in the opposite direction, varying the speed with which they roll their feet and legs to edge the skis (quickly at first and then more gradually).

5. Demonstrate how to aggressively pivot skis, and then, while skidding down the back side of a bump, how to progressively tip the feet, ankles, and knees into the hill while flexing.

    Describe the sensation of control as the skis grip the snow and quickly slow or stop skidding sideways. Swinging the pole during the pivoting helps keep the students moving with their skis; planting the pole as they engage the edges aids in balance as the skis slow down.

6. Allow each member of the

group to try this activity a couple of times, then integrate it into a series of short, pivoted turns through the bumps.

Uphill Christie Garlands

You can have your students use garlands to practice edging, if necessary. Uphill christies which are linked together provide ample opportunity to roll the feet and legs into the hill (engaging the edges) and to rise to release the edges to start down the hill again. If you have terrain available that has small bumps not too close together, you can teach the exercise there. If not, use a groomed section of terrain, then apply the movements to bump skiing.

Demonstrate the following maneuver and then have your students practice it.

1. From the side of the trail, start down and across the hill (at approximately a 45° angle).
2. While flexing at the ankles, knees, and hips, roll your legs into the hill to engage the edges. The skis tips will "pull" you and your skis in an arc back uphill.
3. Before your skis have come to a stop, begin to extend in the ankles, knees, and hips to release the edges. The tips of the skis will start back down the hill.
4. Perform the exercise two or three times before stopping on the far side of the trail.
5. Repeat in the opposite direction.
6. Initiate a full turn with steering. The extension and steering should last approximately to the

fall line. From the fall line to the finish of the turn, try to stop steering and use the uphill christie movement to let the skis finish the turn. Before coming to a stop, extend and steer again so that the process can be repeated during the second half of the next turn.
7. Link these turns together. When having your students try this, keep the practice segment fairly short.

More Exercises for Incorporating Edge- and Pressure-control Skills

Now that the students have learned to apply their skills in the bumps, focus again on expanding their understanding and versatility by playing with different skill blends on groomed terrain.

So far, students have learned to make turns with one sequence of skills—beginning the turn using rotary motion, then adding edge angle as pressure builds and as the turn develops. To expand both their knowledge and their ability to make turns with different skill combinations, explore the idea of lateral learning. Show the students how to make turns using more active edging and pressure–control skills with less emphasis on steering. The size of these turns will become slightly larger while remaining consistently round, and the timing of the movements will be slightly different.

Using Wedge Pedal Turns to Develop Edge- and Pressure-control Skills

Lead your students into consolidating their understanding of skill blending with an exercise called wedge pedals. (This exercise will only take 5 to 10 minutes.) You can teach this exercise with or without poles, based on the skills of your group. If your group exhibits good pole use, then allow them to use poles. If not, they can perform this exercise without poles.

1. On gentle terrain, ask your students to put their skis into a wedge. Some students who have already learned to make parallel turns may be reluctant to ski in a wedge again, so explain that it's only an exercise designed to help them learn more about how to use their skis.
2. Describe the action of pedaling a bicycle—a smooth transition of pressure from one foot to the other as the pedals come around. Using your hands to show what you mean while talking will help emphasize and clarify the idea.
3. Describe how to pedal from one ski to the other while maintaining the wedge. Tell your students not to steer their skis, but to let their skis do the work. Since the skis are already pointing toward a turn (because of the wedge), simply applying pressure—first to one ski and then the other—causes them to turn. Each time they pedal onto a new ski, it

turns, making a small, crescent-shaped turn in the snow.

4. Demonstrate what you just described while skiing toward the group. Highlight the fact that as you pedal onto the ski, you do not try to steer it. Instead, you let the sidecut of the ski make the turn for you! Also, draw attention to your flexion: ankle forward with the leg tipped slightly inward.

5. Repeat the demonstration moving away from the group.

6. Ask your students to try what you've just shown them. This exercise may take a few tries before students can perform it. Be patient with them, because the benefits will be worth the effort. It enables them to make a slicing wedge turn.

Working the Movements into a Parallel Turn

When your group can competently perform wedge pedals, have them work the same movements into a parallel turn. Use fairly flat terrain to help control speed and increase comfort level.

1. In a static position, review the movements of tipping the ankles and knees into the hill while balancing on the downhill ski. This should be a progressive movement during flexion.

2. Make your students aware that they should feel pressure on the big toe and inner side of the ball of the downhill foot as they tip that knee and ankle inward. Explain that this pressure translates into pressure on the edge

of the ski. Skating can be used at this point to help develop these sensations.

Suggest that students press slightly on the front of the boot while flexing to stay centered. This helps them apply consistent pressure throughout the length of the ski.

As the students apply this edging movement to the ski, it begins to turn. They have already experienced this when learning uphill christies.

3. On flat terrain, demonstrate a turn that you initiate with pressure on the big toe and against the edge of the ski. As long as the students remain centered (with pressure on the front of the boot), the design of the ski will pull them into the turn. They should apply pressure during the extension to initiate the turn, and should flex to manage the pressure throughout the rest of the turn (see photo 13).

If the students actively twist or steer their feet and skis, they will be unable to accomplish

the task. Instead, they must focus on creating pressure on the big toe and therefore the edge of the turning ski. Successful performance of this exercise requires solid, well-developed weight transfer.

4. Have your students link a series of these turns together, making sure to keep the group on reasonably flat terrain. Explain to them that when they should use less steering and more active edge and pressure control in their turns.

Since this blend of skills in a turn creates less friction between the skis and the snow, which in turn creates an acceleration, students should use it when they want to maintain their speed on flat, well-groomed terrain. As mentioned previously, they could also use short turns that stay close to the fall line to maintain their speed.

Skiers have to steer more actively on steeper terrain or fresh powder to help control their turn shape. If they try to

Photo 13. Maintaining Pressure in the Front of the Boot

use this type of turn on steeper terrain, they may have difficulty controlling their speed.

Edge- and Pressure-control Awareness through Different Turn Shapes

To help your students more thoroughly understand about using more edging and pressure—and less steering—to turn, have them experiment with different turn shapes. They should continue to flex and tip inward after initiating a turn. Progressive flexion and continued pressure increases edge angle throughout the second half of the turn. This rounds out the bottom of the turn and bring the skis back across the fall line.

Make a game of varying the rate of flexion, applying edging and pressure to make the skis continue to turn. How far can the students turn across the hill before they have slowed down too much to start another turn? How fast can they go while still continuing to turn? Of course, if you play the speed game, be sure that the group is comfortable with going faster, on terrain that deters them from going too fast. These types of games anchor the execution of different skill blends and help students learn how to choose which mechanics to use on a given run or specific type of terrain.

Allow your students enough time during this part of your lesson to apply the concepts of skill blends and turn shapes. The goal is to help students learn to make their own decisions relative to mechanics and turn shapes depending on the terrain and snow conditions. Lead your group to runs that have transitions between steep and flat terrain. Rather than telling them how to ski specific parts of the run, let them choose for themselves. Make yourself available to answer questions and provide suggestions and feedback, if necessary. This portion of any lesson can be especially fun and rewarding for both you and your students.

Powder: Progression for Turn Shape and Skill Blend

Skiing in a few inches of new snow will be great fun for students at this level. Explain to them that the added resistance of deeper snow makes it necessary to apply active steering movements in a consistent, progressive manner. Students at this level may begin to open their skis into a wedge again when they encounter powder snow. Encourage them to stand a little more on both feet and to actively twist both skis toward the new turn. This two-footed stance makes it easier for them to turn both skis simultaneously and enhances their balance at the same time.

If your students experience difficulty initiating the turn, teach them to unweight more aggressively to help get their skis up out of the deeper snow and make them easier to turn. Show the group how to bounce on their skis in a traverse and then give them a chance to practice what you've shown them.

1. Start by dropping or quickly flexing in the ankles and knees.

2. Next, extend quickly and powerfully. As the extension movement slows and you stop moving up, you will feel as though your body hangs momentarily at the top of the extension.

3. Repeat this movement two or three times during a traverse to create a "bouncing" sensation. Each time you bounce back up, the skis are closer to the surface of the snow.

4. On the third bounce, twist both feet toward the next turn. Getting the turn started is the hardest part for students. Once initiated, is reasonably easy to keep the skis turning. If your students still find it difficult to initiate turns in powder, use the wedge pedal exercise (from earlier in this section) to teach them to blend steering with edge and pressure control.

Emphasize active weight transfer through pedaling. More patience at the top of the turn is helpful as well. Have your students powerfully twist the foot and tip the leg slightly more while flexing during the second half of the turn (tipping contributes to leg rotation). As your students gain confidence, have them reduce the size of the wedge during the pedaling portion of the turn until they are once again linking parallel turns. Be sure they keep the turns close to the fall line and encourage them to pedal onto the new ski as soon as they have left the fall line.

Ice: Progression for Turn Shape and Skill Blend

As hard snow and ice offer less resistance to turning, it is not necessary to steer the skis as actively during turn initiation. The reduced resistance also makes it more difficult to control speed. A round, well-finished turn shape is the best choice for icy conditions.

If terrain is moderate, a medium turn will works to control speed, although the skis tend to stay in the fall line for a relatively long period of time. On steeper slopes, for students who are capable of finishing their turns, you should probably teach shorter turns to control speed, since this type of turn involves less time in the fall line. Whichever type of turn you have your students make, be sure they focus less on steering and more on edge and pressure control. Too much steering at the top of the turn causes excessive skidding. Shorter turns require more active steering to initiate, but be sure that your students do not continue to steer as actively throughout the turn. Instead, have them add pressure to the edge (big toe) side of the downhill foot and tip their legs inward to increase the edge angle.

At the top of the turn, pressing on the big toe while maintaining contact with the boot tongue not only engages the edge of the ski, but it also contributes to a passive steering movement because edging movements involve some leg rotation. Because of the reduced friction between the ski and the snow, this passive steering movement will probably be enough to get the

skis turning, especially in a medium turn. Edging the ski increases pressure, which can be controlled by flexing throughout the rest of the turn. By using edge engagement and pressure–control to carefully control the shape of the turn, the skis skid less, resulting in better control.

Consider using hockey slides to help students find the appropriate blend of steering and skidding on ice.

1. Demonstrate a quick, pivoted initiation to get the skis turning—the friction resulting from the skidding will help control speed. After the speed is checked, progressively tip the legs inward to engage the edges and add shape to the bottom of the turn. Finish the turn with a more aggressive edging movement.
2. Have the students practice pivoting and drifting while progressively engaging the skis' edges. Show them how to flex and tip their legs inward quickly and more aggressively. This quick edging results in a powerful edge–set, creating a solid platform.
3. Have the students create pressure under the ball of the foot by steering and extending toward the fall line.

Icy conditions will no doubt be a challenge for students at this level. Helping them learn to choose the correct tactics (turn shapes and skill blends) will go a long way toward helping

them enjoy the mountain in all conditions.

Technical Aspects of Skill Development

Balancing Movements

Students continue to refine and develop their balance while learning to make parallel turns. Previously, they experienced weighting one foot at a time. Now, for the first time, they are using early weight transfer in the turn and learning to balance on one ski from the top of the turn. They refine their balance even more at turn initiation because skis that are parallel offer slightly less lateral stability than skis that are opened into a wedge.

Skating also develops better balance on one foot. Practicing gliding on one foot further refines this ability. Continued use of an active pole plant aids balance because it offers a third point of contact, which increases the size of the platform. As students learn better pole action while skiing in moguls, the pole remains anchored for a fairly long period of time, resulting in a larger platform through the upper half of the turn. Students enhance their balance by using their poles for static exercises. Skiing in moguls further develops your students' balance as they learn to ski in more varied terrain. Flexion enhances balance in the bumps by lowering the center of mass of the body, making it more stable.

Rotary Movements

Students learn to begin using simultaneous steering movements at the top of the turn. Prior to this level, students still primarily used sequential rotary movements to initiate turns, but were beginning to explore simultaneous movements.

As students at this level improve their flexion and extension movements, they also improve their turning movements because any turning movement they make over a range of motion is more powerful (and therefore easier to execute) than it would be with no range of motion (when the legs are locked in a static position, neither flexing or extending). This concept becomes very important when skiing in ungroomed snow conditions. Students also learn more fine motor control as they learn to guide the ski first from the foot, and then to involve the ankle, knee, and ultimately, the hip. Students also refine inside leg steering as they become familiar with the sensations associated with the inside leg. Skating is especially helpful for developing better inside leg activity because the inside leg is turned more than the outside leg.

Edge–control Movements

The initial work on weight transfer (combined with extension) anchors the idea of using extension to release the edges. As students learn to extend more laterally, they find that the mechanism of edge release becomes easier to use. The blending of rotary and edging skills becomes more integrated at this level of skiing. The act of flexing allows the legs to be tipped inward (which in itself produces some rotary motion), actively engaging the edges during the second half of the turn.

Students refine these tipping movements when they continue to work on hockey stops and uphill christies, and in so doing learn to let the design of the skis create the shape of the turn more. In the case of hockey slides, engaging the edges does not so much add shape to the bottom of the turn as it increases the friction between the skis and the snow. This friction slows the skier down. Wedge pedals help students learn that a combination of edging and the application of pressure will create a turn, which allows them to reduce steering movements in some situations. This concept is anchored as students practice parallel pedals.

Pressure–control Movements

The foot-to-foot movements taught in the first part of the parallel turn progression represent pressure control movements. Early weight transfer is an important fundamental of advanced skiing. Increased edge angles create more pressure on the skis because as the skis are tipped up on edge, and the surface area in contact with the snow is reduced.

Flexion plays an important role in controlling pressure by absorbing some of that increase. As the body moves with the pull of gravity (in flexion), some pressure can be relieved from the skis. Pressure increases as edge angles increase and flexion serves to keep the pressure somewhat constant during the second half of the turn.

The vertical motion produced by extension certainly helps to flatten the ski (making it easier to steer), and when the student applies that motion quickly and powerfully, it results in up-unweighting. Students use up-unweighting to make parallel turns in powder when they learn to bounce while traversing. On groomed snow, especially with modern ski equipment, students usually use extension to release the edges rather than to unweight the skis. In skating, however, instead of extending to release the edges, the student actually holds the ski on edge and extends (pushes) off the ski.

Questions: Parallel Turns

Note: Unless otherwise noted, the following questions concern skills, exercises or progressions appropriate for students at Level 6.

1. Choose one or more of the following:
    If transferring weight to the new outside ski does not help your students initiate a parallel turn, you might want to suggest they:
    A. Keep their weight over the old outside ski for this phase of the turn
    B. Distribute their weight evenly between both skis
    C. Actively extend

2. Choose one or more of the following:
    The study guide describes a static exercise for establishing early weight transfer which consists of having your students shift their weight from foot to foot. Which of the following should they avoid?
    A. Moving their legs and feet but keeping their upper body quiet
    B. Moving their hips and shoulders from side to side as they shift their weight from foot to foot
    C. Pressing down on the foot they wish to weight
    D. Actually lifting the light ski off the snow

3. What reason does the study guide give for having your students flex and extend in the dynamic version of the above weight transfer exercise?

    _____

    _____

4. Choose one or more of the following:
    At this level, you might want to teach students to skate to help:
    A. Develop a more active weight transfer
    B. Develop independent movements of the legs
    C. Develop edge-control movements
    D. Anchor flexion and extension movements

5. Choose one or more of the following:
    Commonly, students have difficulty learning to skate because:
    A. They over–edge their skis
    B. They do not edge the ski from which they are pushing off enough
    C. They do not flex their ankles enough
    D. They flex their ankles too much
    E. None of the above

6. Under what conditions does the study guide suggest using poles in a Level 6 skating lesson?

    _____

7. Why is it easier to turn your foot and ski when you lift them off of the snow?

_____

8. Choose the best answer:
   When turning, you should:
   A. Start to turn from the foot, then involve the leg
   B. Start to turn from the leg, then involve the foot
   C. Start to turn from the hip, then involve the leg

9. Define fine motor control.

_____

10. After each of the following statements, write "one-at-a-time" or "task."

   A. Easier to provide feedback for each student. _____

   B. Easier to check each individual's understanding. _____

   C. Requires you to watch everyone for a few turns each, and to remember how well each person

      executed the task so that you can provide feedback when you regroup. _____

   D. You give each individual a personal focus (relative to their personal needs),

      then choose and identify a place to regroup (such as a bend or a flat spot in a trail). _____

   E. The group has to stand longer in one place on the hill. _____

   F. Gives everyone the chance to try combining the movements you have taught them. _____

   G. Can place unnecessary pressure on some people because they feel everyone is watching them!

      _____

11. Circle the best choice:
    At this level, you should teach your students to transfer their weight to their new ski
    (before) / (after) they have used their foot and leg to steer into the turn.

12. Choose the best answer.
    During a parallel turn, on what part of their outside foot should students at this level feel pressure?
    A. Inner side (big toe side) of the ball of the foot
    B. Outer side (little toe side) of the ball of the foot
    C. Middle of the ball of the foot

13. Choose the best answer:
    During a parallel turn, on what part of their inside foot should students at this level feel pressure?
    A. Inner side (big toe side) of the ball of the foot
    B. Outer side (little toe side) of the ball of the foot
    C. Middle of the ball of the foot

14. The study guide contains a static exercise for teaching how it feels to actively steer the inside foot in a parallel turn. The first two steps are included below. Describe the rest of the exercise in the space provided.
    A. Stand statically with your skis perpendicular to the fall line on relatively flat terrain.
    B. Place the tips of your poles in the snow on either side of you for balance
       (The downhill pole should be next to the downhill ski, just in front of the toe piece).

    C. _____

    D. _____

15. The study guide describes an alternative way to place one of the ski poles in the above inside foot steering exercise. What is this alternative and why might you use it?

    _____

    _____

    _____

16. What is the small group style of teaching?

    _____

    _____

17. Define lateral extension:

    _____

    _____

    _____

18. True or false:
    On groomed snow with modern ski equipment, extension is usually used to release the edges instead of to unweight the skis.

19. The study guide suggests introducing lateral movements after your group can already make parallel turns. Why?

   _____

20. Circle the best choice for each of the questions below:
   The first few steps of the bull's eye progression are:
   Step 1:   Draw a bull's eye in the snow.
   Step 2:   Place your downhill ski pole in the snow to support your body and help you to balance. The point of the pole should be in line with the (heel piece) / (toe piece) of your binding and far enough downhill so you can use it as a brace of sorts.
   Step 3:   Lean on the pole and lift the (downhill) / (uphill) foot a few inches off the ground without beginning to extend.
   Step 4:   Extend towards the bull's eye. As you begin to extend, use the whole leg to push your hip toward the bull's eye while gradually twisting the new (inside) / (outside) ski. The edge will release, and the ski will start down the hill.

21. Circle the best choice:
   To begin a cowboy turn, actively tip your (inside) / (outside) knee down the hill.

22. Choose one or more of the following:
   Which of the following is/are most appropriate for teaching simultaneous steering:
   A.   Cowboy turns
   B.   Hockey slides
   C.   Patience turns
   D.   Skating
   E.   Thousand steps

23. Choose one or more of the following:
   Before actually having your students ski on bumps for the first time, you might want to have them try to pivot (statically) on a bump. To help keep the skis relatively flat:
   A.   The hips should be angulated into the hill and the upper body should be angulated down the hill
   B.   The hips should be angulated into the hill and the upper body should be aligned over the feet
   C.   The hips and upper body should be angulated into the hill
   D.   The hips and upper body should be aligned over the feet

24. Choose the best answer:
   When learning to ski in moguls, which of the following can help keep you centered as you slide off the bump:
   A.   Pressuring the back cuff of the boot
   B.   Pressuring the front tongue of the boot
   C.   Neither of the above

25. The study guide mentions several advantages for having your Level 6 students plant their poles fairly early.

   Name one of these. _____

26. Circle the best choice:
    In a beginning pole planting lesson in the bumps, students should remove the pole they have planted (prior to skiing past the insertion point) / (after they have skied past the insertion point).

27. Circle the best choice:
    After planting their pole, students should hinge at the (elbow) / (wrist) to keep from dropping the inside hand.

28. Initially, to help your beginning bump students learn when to start to steer their skis down the hill, you could tell them to start steering as soon as they see what piece of their equipment reach the crest of the bump?

    _____

29. Choose one or more of the following:
    Steering your feet and skis more aggressively as you come over the top of a bump:
    A. Should be avoided
    B. Will lengthen the turn
    C. Will shorten the turn
    D. Will not affect the size of the turn

30. Choose one or more of the following:
    The pedal wedge turns described in the study guide are primarily designed to help develop which of the following movements:
    A. Edge coontrol
    B. Pressure control
    C. Rotary

31. Choose one or more of the following:
    When students tip the outside knee and ankle inward in a parallel pedal turn:
    A. They should feel pressure on the big toe and inner side of the ball of the foot
    B. They should feel pressure on the little toe and outer side of the ball of the foot
    C. This will pressure the edge of the ski

32. Circle the best choice:
    Turns with more active edge and pressure control and less steering and will create (less) / (more) friction between the skis and the snow, thus creating an acceleration.

33. Circle the best choice:
    All else being equal, will you have to steer (less actively) or (more actively) in powder than in hard packed snow?

34. Circle the best choice:
    All else being equal, will you have to steer (less actively) or (more actively) on a steep slope than on a less steep slope?

35. Circle the best choice:
    Continuing to flex down and inward after initiating a turn will (decrease) / (increase) edge angles
    through the second half of a turn.

36. Circle the best choice:
    Because deeper snow offers (less) / (more) resistance, you should apply active steering movements
    in a consistent, progressive manner.

37. Choose one or more of the following:
    Some Level 6 students tend to open their skis into a wedge when they encounter powder snow. To make it
    easier for them to turn both skis simultaneously in powder, you might want to have them:
    A.   Practice pedal wedge turns
    B.   Begin their turns by actively shifting their weight to the new outside turning ski
    C.   Stand a little more on both feet and actively twist both skis toward the new turn

38. Choose one or more of the following:
    To help students who are having difficulty initiating turns in powder, have them try:
    A.   Unweighting more gradually
    B.   Unweighting more aggressively
    C.   Powder bounces
    D.   Pedal wedge exercises

39. Circle the best choice:
    In powder, you should use more patience at the (top) / (bottom) of the turn.

40. Circle the best choice:
    Ice offers (less) / (more) resistance to turning.

41. Choose the best answer:
    Which type of turn does the study guide recommend having your students use to control their speed on
    steeper, icy slopes? (Assume that your students are capable of finishing all three of the following turn
    types equally well)
    A.   Short
    B.   Medium
    C.   Long

42. Circle the best choice:
    A medium–radius turn involves (less) / (more) time in the fall line than a shorter turn.

43. Circle the best choice:
    Medium–radius turns require you to steer (more) / (less) actively during turn initiation
    than shorter radius turns do.

44. Circle the best choice:
    On ice, too much steering at the top of the turn will cause (edge lock) / (excessive skidding).

45. Which exercise/activity described in the study guide is an exception to the idea that extending is used to release the edges?

_____

46. Read the following descriptions of movements and skills that were introduced or refined during the Level 6 lesson and then write the name of the fundamental skill primarily involved. (Fundamental skills: Balance, Rotary, Edge Control, Pressure Control)
Note: If part of the description has been bolded, write the name of the fundamental skill which primarily applies to that portion of the description.

A. Flexion enhances this skill in the bumps by lowering the center of mass of the body, making it more stable. _____

B. Skating is especially helpful for developing better inside leg activity because the inside leg is turned more than the outside leg. _____

C. As students at this level become better at flexion and extension movements, they **improve their turning movements** because any turning movement they make over a range of motion is more powerful (and therefore easier to execute) than the same movement made when there is no range of motion (when the legs are locked in a static position, neither flexing further nor extending more). _____

D. The foot-to-foot movements taught in the first part of the parallel turn progression represent this skill. Early weight transfer is an important fundamental of advanced skiing. _____

E. Students refine this skill even more at turn initiation because skis that are parallel offer slightly less lateral stability than skis that are opened into a wedge. _____

F. As students learn to extend more laterally, they find that the mechanism of edge release becomes easier to use. _____

G. Students also refine inside leg steering as they become familiar with the sensations associated with the inside leg, and thus learn to control the degree to they steer the inside leg._____

H. Continued use of an active pole plant offers a third point of contact, which increases the size of the platform. As students learn better pole action while skiing in moguls, the pole remains anchored for a fairly long period of time, resulting in a larger platform through the upper half of the turn. Students enhance this fundamental skill by using their poles for static exercises.

_____

I. Students learn to use simultaneous steering movements beginning at the top of the turn. Prior to this level, students still used sequential movements to initiate turns, but were beginning to explore simultaneous movements later in the turn. _____

J. Increasing the edge angle creates more pressure on the skis because as the skis are tipped up on edge, the surface area in contact with the snow is reduced. _____

K. Students use up–unweighting to make parallel turns in powder when they learn to bounce while traversing. _____

Level 6 Answers: Parallel Turns

1. B & C. If transferring the weight to the new outside ski does not work very well for a particular group, you could try introducing a parallel turn with equal weight on both feet. Using the terrain and/or very active flexion and extension movements will facilitate the unweighting and edge release of the skis and will make it possible to initiate a parallel turn.

2. B. To perform the static exercise described in the study guide for establishing early weight transfer, students should press down on the foot they wish to weight. It may be helpful to have them actually lift the light ski off the snow during this exercise. If they are having difficulty with this exercise, watch to make sure that they are not moving their hips and shoulders from side to side as they shift their weight from foot to foot. (The transfer of weight should come from movements of the legs and feet underneath a quiet upper body.)

3. Facilitates the weight transfer. Flexing and extending in the dynamic version of the weight transfer exercise *facilitates the weight transfer* and also helps anchor the idea that flexion and extension are an integral and fundamental part of skiing!

4. A, B, C, & D.

5. B & C. Commonly, students have difficulty learning to skate because:
    * of a lack of edge engagement
    * they are standing too tall and without sufficient flex in the ankle

6. If at least some members of the group already use pole plants in their turns. You might want to include a pole plant in a Level 6 skating lesson *if at least some members of your group are using a pole plant when they turn.* Try not to emphasize pole use too much because it may detract from students' ability to focus on the newer elements you are teaching.

7. Because there's no resistance from the snow. When turning a lifted ski, *there is no resistance from the snow.*

8. A. Starting to turn skis from the feet first, then involving the rest of the leg for more power is important for beginning to learn *fine motor control*—the ability to refine and control movements with different parts of their bodies.

9. Fine motor control is *the ability to refine and control movements with different parts of your body.*

10. A. *One–at–a–time.* Easier to provide feedback for each student.
    B. *One–at–a–time.* Easier to check each individual's understanding.
    C. *Task.* Requires you to watch everyone for a few turns each, and to remember how well each person executed the task so that you can provide feedback when you regroup.
    D. *Task.* You give each individual a personal focus (relative to their personal needs), then choose and identify a place to regroup (such as a bend or a flat spot in a trail).
    E. *One–at–a–time.* The group has to stand longer in one place on the hill.
    F. *Task.* Gives everyone the chance to try combining the movements you have taught them.
    G. *One–at–a–time.* Can place unnecessary pressure on some people because they feel everyone is watching them!

11. Before. In Level 6, your students learn to transfer weight to their new ski *before* using the foot and leg to guide that ski into the new turn. Flexion and extension movements will aid in balance and make steering the new ski easier.

12. A. While steering the feet in a Level 6 parallel turn, a student at this level should feel a sensation of pressure on the inner (big toe) side of the ball of the foot where it touches the inside of the ski boot.

13. B. To steer the inside ski, create similar pressure on the outer (little toe) side of the ball of the foot inside the ski boot.

14. C.   Lift the downhill ski off the snow.
    D.   Twist the foot by pressing the little toe side of the ball of the downhill foot against the pole. You will feel added resistance to twisting the ski. This resistance will highlight the sensation of actively turning the inside foot.
        If you tip your downhill knee down the hill as well while twisting your foot at the same time, you will feel you can exert more power against your ski pole.
        This exercise will give your students an idea of how it feels to steer their inside foot in a parallel turn.

15. Inserting the uphill pole in the snow between the tails of your skis. An alternative way to use your uphill ski pole in the above exercise is to *put it in the snow between the tails of your skis to* provide even more resistance.

16. Working with a few people at a time. The *small group* style involves *working with a few people at a time* while keeping everyone moving and focused. After part of a run, you should rotate to another group so that after one or two runs you will have worked with each of the small groups. This style allows your students to interact and ski in a structured, yet more relaxed setting.

17. Extending down the hill and toward the new turn. Lateral extension is using the extension to make the body move more *down the hill* and *toward* the new turn (lateral extension), rather than vertically and away from the new turn.

18. True. On groomed snow, especially with modern ski equipment, extension is used to release the edges more often than to unweight the skis.

19. Can reduce the intimidation factor. Moving the body more down the hill than upward can be intimidating. To minimize the intimidation factor, introduce lateral movements after your group can already make parallel turns. Students who can already make parallel turns will *know* that their skis will turn when they transfer their weight and steer both feet. They will quickly realize that extending by moving their hips slightly forward and across their skis makes it even easier to initiate the turn.

20. In line with the toe piece, downhill, hip, outside.
    The bull's eye extension progression:
    Step 1:   Draw a bull's eye in the snow.
    Step 2:   Place your downhill ski pole in the snow to support your body and help you to balance. The point of the pole should be *in line with the toe piece* and far enough downhill so you can use it as a brace of sorts.

Step 3:   Lean on the pole and lift the *downhill* foot a few inches off the ground without
           beginning to extend.

Step 4:   Extend towards the bull's eye. As you begin to extend, use the whole leg to push
           your hip toward the bull's eye while gradually twisting the new *outside* ski.
           The edge will release, and the ski will start down the hill.

21.   Inside. In a cowboy turn, you are to imagine the bowlegged appearance of a cowboy's legs: there is more
       space between his knees than his feet. The goal is to make your legs look bowlegged as you start the turn
       by actively tipping your *inside* knee down the hill.

22.   A, B, & C. Cowboy Turns, hockey slides, and patience turns can help your students learn to
       steer their skis simultaneously.

23.   D. Because so little of the ski is in contact with the snow, it is easy to get the skis to pivot on top of a bump.
       The hips and upper body should *remain aligned over the feet* to help keep the skis relatively flat on the
       snow. Try to pivot your skis by creating pressure against the inside of your ski boots with the balls of your
       feet. The inner side of the uphill foot and the outer side of the downhill foot should press against the inside
       of the boot so that both ski tips travel in the same direction.

24.   B. A little bit of forward pressure on the boot tongue can help keep you centered as you slide off the bump
       (the skis will tend to accelerate slightly as they slide down the back of the bump).

25.   Draws the body into the turn and provides another point of contact, which improves balance and provides a
       sense of security.
           Having your students swing the pole as they initiate a turn will help draw their bodies forward and
       down the hill as they begin to turn, and will leave the pole in a ready position so that it can be planted as
       they ski up on top of the next mogul.
           Although the reduced ski–snow contact (on top of the bump) makes the skis easy to steer, it also
       reduces the platform. Adding the pole plant at that point will improve balance and the sense of security by
       adding another point of contact during an otherwise unstable period of turn initiation.

26.   After they have skied past the insertion point. In a beginning pole planting lesson in the bumps, students
       should remove the pole they have planted *after they have skied past the insertion point.*

27.   Wrist. Once your students have skied past the spot where they have planted the pole, they should hinge at
       the *wrist* to keep from dropping the inside hand.

28.   The toe piece of the binding. As a visual cue about where on the bump to start twisting or pivoting, tell your
       students to start steering their skis down the hill as soon as they see the *toe piece of the binding* reach the
       crest of the bump.
           As they get a sense for this timing, encourage them to begin to rely on watching the skis less and less
       and to substitute feeling the bump with the soles of their feet instead.

29.   C. Simply having your group make a series of turns where they steer their feet and skis more aggressively as
       they come over the top of the bump will lead to a shorter turn.

30. A & B. Pedal wedge turns are primarily designed to develop edge and pressure control skills.

31. A & C. Make your students aware that in a parallel turn they should feel pressure on both their big toe and on the inner side (of the ball of the outside or turning) foot as they tip that knee and ankle inward. Explain that this pressure will translate into pressure on the edge of the ski.

32. Less. Since turns with less steering and more active edge and pressure control will create *less* friction between the skis and the snow, thus creating an acceleration, students will find this type of turn appropriate when they want to maintain their speed on flat, well-groomed terrain. They could also use short turns that stay close to the fall line to maintain their speed.

33. More actively. All else being equal, you will have to steer more actively in powder than in hard packed snow.

34. More actively. All else being equal, you will have to steer more actively on steeper slopes.

35. Increase. Having your students continue to flex both down and inward after initiating a turn will *increase* the edge angle through the second half of the turn. Progressive flexion and continued pressure will round out the bottom of the turn and bring the skis back across the fall line.

36. More. Because of the *added* resistance of the deeper snow, it is necessary to apply active steering movements in a consistent, progressive manner.

37. C. To help your Level 6 students turn both skis simultaneously in powder snow, have them stand a little more on both feet and actively twist both skis toward the new turn. The more two–footed stance will make it easier for them to turn both skis simultaneously, and will enhance their balance at the same time.

38. B, C, & D. If Level 6 students are experiencing difficulty initiating a turn in powder, you might want to teach them to unweight more aggressively to help them get their skis up out of the deeper snow and make the skis easier to turn. The powder bounce progression outlined in the study guide teaches this. If powder bounces don't help, the study guide suggests using the wedge pedal exercise (described prior to the powder section in Level 6) to help your students blend steering with edge and pressure in powder snow. For powder, try emphasizing an active weight transfer through pedaling. Have them twist the foot more powerfully and tip the leg a little more while flexing during the second half of the turn (tipping will contribute to the rotation of the leg).

39. Top. In powder, use more patience at the top of the turn.

40. Less. Since hard snow and ice offer *less* resistance to turning, it is not necessary to steer the skis as actively during turn initiation. Also, the reduced resistance makes it more difficult to control speed.

41. A. The study guide suggests that, for students who are capable of finishing their shorter–radius turns, a *shorter* turn may be a better choice for steeper, icy slopes because this type of turn involves less time in the fall line.

42. More. You are in the fall line for a *longer* period of time during a medium–radius turn than you are for a short–radius turn, which is why the study guide recommends having your students use a shorter turn for steep, icy slopes—*provided that they can finish their turns.*

43.   Less. Medium–radius turns don't require you to steer as actively during turn initiation as shorter radius turns do.

44.   Excessive skidding. On ice, too much steering at the top of the turn will cause the skis to skid excessively. The study guide suggests that for shorter turns, you have your students follow the active steering movement necessary to initiate the turn with pressuring the edge (big toe) and tipping the legs inward to increase the edge angle.

45.   *Skating* is an exception to the idea that extending is used to release the edges. In skating, pressure increases during extension because the ski is held on edge as the skier pushes off of it.

46.   A.   Balance. Flexion enhances balance in the bumps by lowering the center of mass of the body, making it more stable.

       B.   Rotary movement: Skating is especially helpful for developing better inside leg activity because the inside leg is turned more than the outside leg.

       C.   Rotary movement: As students at this level become better at flexion and extension movements, they improve their turning movements because any turning movement they make over a range of motion is more powerful (and therefore easier to execute) than the same movement made when there is no range of motion (when the legs are locked in a static position, neither flexing further nor extending more).

       D.   Pressure–control movement: The foot–to–foot movements taught in the first part of the parallel turn progression represent this skill. Early weight transfer is an important fundamental of advanced skiing.

       E.   Balance: Students refine their balance even more at turn initiation because skis that are parallel offer slightly less lateral stability than skis that are opened into a wedge.

       F.   Edge–control movement: As students learn to extend more laterally, they find that the mechanism of edge release becomes easier to use.

       G.   Rotary movement: Students also refine inside leg steering as they become familiar with the sensations associated with the inside leg, and thus learn to control the degree to they steer the inside leg.

       H.   Balance: Continued use of an active pole plant aids balance because it offers a third point of contact, which increases the size of the platform. As students learn better pole action while skiing in moguls, the pole remains anchored for a fairly long period of time, resulting in a larger platform through the upper half of the turn. Students enhance their balance by using their poles for static exercises.

       I.   Rotary movement: Students learn to use simultaneous steering movements beginning at the top of the turn. Prior to this level, students still used sequential rotary movements to initiate turns, but were beginning to explore simultaneous movements later in the turn.

       J.   Pressure–control movement: Increasing the edge angle creates more pressure on the skis because as the skis are tipped up on edge, the surface area in contact with the snow is reduced.

       K.   Pressure–control movement: Students use up unweighting to make parallel turns in powder when they learn to bounce while traversing.

Notes:

Notes: